Adrift: America in 100 Charts

ALSO BY SCOTT GALLOWAY

Post Corona: From Crisis to Opportunity

*The Algebra of Happiness: Notes on the
Pursuit of Success, Love, and Meaning*

*The Four: The Hidden DNA of Amazon,
Apple, Facebook, and Google*

Adrift:
America in
100 Charts

Scott Galloway

PORTFOLIO | PENGUIN

PORTFOLIO / PENGUIN
An imprint of Penguin Random House LLC
penguinrandomhouse.com

Most Portfolio books are available at a discount when purchased in quantity for sales promotions or
corporate use. Special editions, which include personalized covers, excerpts, and corporate imprints,
can be created when purchased in large quantities. For more information, please call (212) 572-2232
or email specialmarkets@penguinrandomhouse.com. Your local bookstore can also assist with
discounted bulk purchases using the Penguin Random House corporate Business-to-Business program.
For assistance in locating a participating retailer, email B2B@penguinrandomhouse.com.

Chapter art © Luba Lukova
Charts and graphs by Prof G Media. Used with permission.

ISBN 9780593542408 (hardcover)
ISBN 9780593542415 (ebook)

Printed in the United States of America
2nd Printing

BOOK DESIGN BY OLIVIA REANEY-HALL

For my cousin Andrew Levene, who died of Covid-19 complications at 52.

Contents

2. The World We Made

8. The Bright Side of Instability

9. Possible Futures

Adrift: America in 100 Charts

Ballast

Life isn't what happens to you, but how you react to what happens to you. Nations prosper or perish based on how they respond to crises.

Preface: Ballast

We are a nation adrift. We lack neither wind nor sail, we have no shortage of captains or gear, yet our mighty ship flounders in a sea of partisanship, corruption, and selfishness. Our discourse is coarse, young people are failing to form relationships, and our brightest seek individual glory at the expense of the commonwealth. Our institutions are decaying, and the connective tissue of society frays nearly beyond repair. On the horizon, darkness and thunder. To the west, China rises. In the east, Europe fades.

What will it take to turn this vessel before the wind and plot a course for peace and prosperity? OK, enough with the sailing metaphors. I can't tell a mainsail from a jib, but I do know how to read a chart. There's something powerful about the visual representation of data; it reaches our instinctive ability to assess by sight vs. the intellectual exercise of reading words and data. For years now, I've been talking to people on my podcasts, in business, and at NYU, where I teach, about the state of America and where we're headed. Over and over, I find that data clarifies those conversations, helps me see things clearer. So when I decided to collect my views on this essential question of America's sputtering progress, it seemed natural to do it with charts front and center.

What the data tells me is not complicated: America is a work in progress, but it's made the most progress toward its ideals, it's become the most like itself, when it has invested in a strong middle class. There, that's my grand economic theory. What

makes me so sure about this? The data. And the story that
data tells.

That story begins nearly eighty years ago. In the summer of 1945,
the most destructive event in humanity's long history of violence
came to an end. Nazi Germany collapsed in April, and in August,
after the U.S. dropped two atomic bombs, Imperial Japan
surrendered. Nations devastated by battle would take a generation
to rebuild. The U.S. faced a different problem.

Though American soil saw little combat, the war transformed
the U.S. economy. The automobile industry retooled to build
tanks and planes. Shipping and internal transportation were
reconfigured to support armament production and transport.
Rations limited the consumption of goods ranging from gasoline
to soap. In 1945, 40% of the nation's GDP was directed to the war
effort. (Today, we spend 3.7% of our GDP on the military.) The
U.S., in a deep depression before the war, had been reanimated
into a purpose-built economy, Roosevelt's "Arsenal
of Democracy."

With the arrival of peace, that purpose dissipated. The economy
lost the customer responsible for almost half of its business.
Tank factories and shipping depots closed; over the following
twenty-four months, the U.S. military shed 10 million service
members. Ten million people, mostly young men, needed jobs,
homes, cars, and ... prospects.

When the ticker tape parades finished, wages began to fall and rents began to rise. Workers in every major industry went on strike, and a nationalist movement began bubbling up from the simmering belief that we'd overinvested abroad at the expense of domestic needs. Planners feared that the economy would return to the pre-war Depression, or worse.

Except that's not what happened. Instead, the arsenal of democracy transformed into the engine of capitalism. The next thirty years brought record-low unemployment, sustained economic growth, and widespread investment in infrastructure and R&D.

The leap forward in the human condition was breathtaking, and not just in the U.S. Infant mortality and poverty plummeted worldwide, and life expectancy and literacy skyrocketed. A global effort, largely funded and led by the U.S., eradicated smallpox. The disease that had killed 90% of Indigenous Americans became the first to be eradicated by human intent. In 1969, three brave astronauts traveled 240,000 miles (note: approximately 3,600 times farther than Blue Origin's *New Shepard*), and an American set foot on Earth's only natural satellite.

The Rise of the Middle Class

How did this happen? Much has been made of the "Greatest Generation," the men and women whose character was forged by the struggles of the 1930s and '40s and who are credited with building the economic colossus America, Inc.

But greatness is in the agency of others. Workers joined unions to secure higher wages and safer conditions. Membership grew in organizations from the Girl Scouts to Kiwanis. Societal connective tissue grew and strengthened. Team sports and little leagues became neighborhood fixtures and multimillion-dollar enterprises.

Underlying this prosperity was robust state support. The G.I. Bill funded college for 2 million soldiers and home loans and small business loans for hundreds of thousands more. Truman's housing legislation expanded the government's role in building homes and financing home ownership. Eisenhower launched a forty-year project to build a national highway system, at a cost of over $500 billion in today's dollars. Income taxes were progressive—the top rate was 91%—and the wealth of the biggest earners was redistributed through social programs and investments in infrastructure, education, and science.

The years after World War II were an era of great innovation—the computer, the cellular phone, and the internet are all products of the postwar period. But the U.S.'s greatest innovation was not a thing, it was a social and economic construct: the middle class.

A broad, inclusive, and prosperous middle class provided capitalism something it had long lacked: ballast. Sorry, just one more nautical metaphor. Ballast is a heavy material—beneath the surface, invisible—that provides stability to a boat. The more tumultuous the environment, the more important the ballast. The absence of this steadying force increases the likelihood a ship will capsize, regardless of the value of the contents sitting above the surface.

In the 1950s and '60s, we had ballast. The combination of wage growth, public education, economic mobility, and an abundance of manufactured goods brought an unprecedented quality of life to millions of households. The term "working class" couldn't encompass the two-car garage, summer vacations, and son (and soon, daughter) heading off to college that exemplified an American middle-class lifestyle. It was an expansive concept: The doctor, lawyer, and Madison Avenue ad man lived a life of greater luxury than their factory worker countrymen, but they had more in common than ever before. The middle class represented the obliteration of class as a concept: Today, somewhere around 70% of Americans describe themselves as middle class.

The U.S. still had too many poor people and a few mega-millionaires, but for a multiple-decade run in the middle of the century, one group defined the cultural and economic narrative of the American story, and it wasn't "innovators" worth the GDP of a Central American nation. As a group, the middle class valued stability, believed in progress, and witnessed firsthand the possibility of widely distributed prosperity. Capitalism, which had a mixed history for all but the capitalists themselves, was proving it could, when steadied by the ballast of a broad middle class, create a rich and healthy society.

Contrary to perception, the postwar middle class was not solely the province of white men. Twenty-seven million American women entered the workforce between 1950 and 1980, increasing their participation by 50%. In 1940, just 22% of Black men were in the middle class by income, compared to 38% of white men. By 1970, 68% of Black men were earning a middle-class income, compared to 65% of white men. America had not overcome its founding inequities, but it had made greater progress against them than in any other period.

New Crises

By the 1970s, however, the nation's run of success was faltering. Access to middle-class prosperity expanded in the postwar period, but it fell short at the upper end of the middle class and beyond—high-earning professions including law, medicine, and senior corporate roles remained overwhelmingly white and male. Poverty and limited opportunities persisted in communities and across generations. As economic growth slowed in the 1960s and '70s, patience for inequity wore thin, and the bonds of postwar prosperity began to fray. The limits of the civil rights movement's progress illuminated the significant remaining obstacles standing in the way of a United States.

Likewise, the dynamism and innovation of the immediate postwar era began to lose energy. Conglomerates became the rage in corporate America, a misguided effort by senior management to insulate themselves, and their incomes, from the risks and volatility of a capitalist (i.e., competitive) marketplace. The environmental costs of industrial expansion produced places such as Love Canal, a neighborhood near Niagara Falls so contaminated by industrial waste that 1,000 families had to be relocated. The arrival of superior Japanese cars on American roads revealed that our manufacturing base had lost its way. And the nation that had saved the world for democracy found itself supporting autocrats to keep the next domino from falling.

In 1980, as in 1945, fearful predictions of national demise cued a fierce debate over the future course of the American experiment. Our response to that period of national crisis, like our response to the challenges of the postwar era, created the America we've inherited today, four decades later.

This book is about that response, the America it produced, and where we may go from here.

Just as in 1945 and 1980, we are once again a nation at a crossroads. We're emerging, slowly, from a pandemic that has killed more than a million Americans as it becomes endemic. Our exceptional technologies—computers we carry in our pockets, instant communication with anyone around the world—bring with them exceptional externalities that our laws, tax code, and culture seem ill-equipped to handle.

Marginalized voices and an entrenched white patriarchy seem to be preparing for war rather than seeking common ground. We have tremendous prosperity but little progress, as more of the spoils accrue to fewer parties.

These 100 charts tell the story of how we got here, and where we might head. To be clear, we're not using charts because they confer objectivity or infallibility. We have chosen data and representations of it that tell the story of America as we see it. But there is a clarity to illustrations and graphs that prose can't match. Our mission is simple: present visuals that strike a chord and inspire action.

CHAPTER 1

Rise of the Shareholder Class

As the postwar boom began to fizzle out, the U.S. embraced shareholder capitalism and turned from community and institution toward rugged individualism.

Following the crises and convulsions of the 1960s and '70s, a new religion emerged in America: shareholder value. Under its precepts, the operations of a corporation were gauged by a single metric: the price of its shares. By extension, the whole society could be evaluated by the aggregate share prices of its corporations. Wall Street became our church, and the Dow Jones and Nasdaq our liturgy.

It was an appropriate metric for a digital age. Just as CDs replaced vinyl, shareholder value reduced the noise of analog ideas, such as community and commonwealth, to a binary up-or-down share price. Red or green, bear or bull.

Shareholder value's high priest, Milton Friedman, declared that executives who made decisions on grounds other than increasing share price were *stealing* from shareholders and "preaching pure and unadulterated socialism." Or worse, you could be accused of being European.

My first job out of UCLA in the 1980s was in the analyst program at Morgan Stanley. Like most of my analyst class, I had no idea what investment banking was, only that we were at the helm of the capitalist bobsled and could make a lot of money. There was scant consideration to the role finance played in society (or whether you'd find the work rewarding). We were charged with birthing the apex predator of the capitalist species, the public company. What we did was noble—we were making money helping other people raise money so they could invest money to ... wait for it ... make more money.

Ronald Reagan's election in 1980 cemented this ethos in government policy. In his inaugural address, he drew battle lines: "In this present crisis, government is not the solution to our problem; government is the problem." In his presentation of American decline, labor and government had allied to suppress the shareholder class, producing an anemic economy that threatened the freedom to be successful. Reagan moved quickly to end the government's restrictions on American economic might: high taxes on our most productive citizens, overregulation of business, and the beast of entitlement programs gnawing at the roots of capitalism. The Gipper ripped out "liberalism" and replaced it with rugged individualism and the "right to dream heroic dreams."

The results were impressive. The economy roared, growing every year of his presidency but one, and inflation fell from 14% to 4%. In an ascending era of shareholder value, the Dow Jones Industrial Average, which had been drifting downward since the mid-1960s, doubled.

Of course, Reagan had the wind at his back. The Soviet Union's collapse and China's transition to a market economy opened vast new markets and cheap labor to supply them. This, coupled with technological innovation that had been percolating in research laboratories, was the gangster capital driving a series of leaps forward, from industrial automation to personal computing, that only accelerated in the post-Reagan years. Waves of technological transitions kick-started societal change and inspired trillions of dollars in economic growth.

Trickle-Down Tax Plan

The signature policy tool of the Reagan era was the tax cut. When he took office, the highest marginal tax rate was 70%—which was the lowest it had been since 1935. When he passed the baton to his vice president, George H. W. Bush, that rate was 28%.

The top marginal rate is not the ultimate determinant of taxes paid, and economists debate the precise impact of the many changes to tax brackets and deductions throughout this time. But the objective of the cuts was met: to reduce the taxes paid by the wealthiest individuals and the largest corporations. In theory, money not spent on taxes was to be "reinvested" into the economy to spur growth, benefitting all.

How well that theory held up in practice is also the subject of significant debate. One thing is certain: The Reagan tax cuts ensured the largest federal deficits since WWII. When Reagan took office, the government owed $930 billion. When he left, the debt was $2.7 trillion. No other peacetime president has tripled the debt. More damaging, Reagan tapped into an emerging lack of long-term thinking in America. Dick Cheney summarized it, observing that "Reagan proved deficits don't matter." And they haven't, until they will. The U.S. national debt now threatens to exceed $30 trillion, and the ratio of debt to GDP, which was 32% when Reagan was sworn in, has exploded to over 120% today.

01

Top Marginal Tax Rates

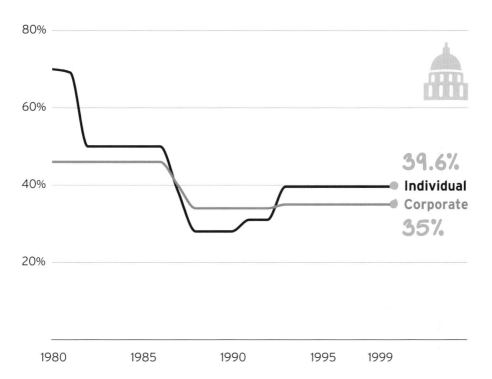

Sources: Tax Foundation (Corporate), Tax Policy Center (Individual).

Changing Sentiments

Political rhetoric is a decent barometer of the ideological state of the nation, and rhetoric changed markedly in the Reagan Revolution. We lost sight of some of the principal reasons for government: to protect the rights of the minority against the majority; to invest in things the market doesn't like paying for, like education, infrastructure, and deep research; and to provide a safety net for those who slip through the cracks of the capitalist marketplace. Many came to see government as a threat to liberty, not its protector.

It didn't use to be this way. Throughout the first half of the twentieth century, investing in our democracy was seen as a patriotic duty. In 1953, General Motors President Charlie Wilson famously said that what was good for our country was good for General Motors, and vice versa. "The difference," he said, "did not exist." Not paying taxes was committing self-harm, because our government was a reflection of ourselves, a representative democracy.

02

Presidential Statements on Government

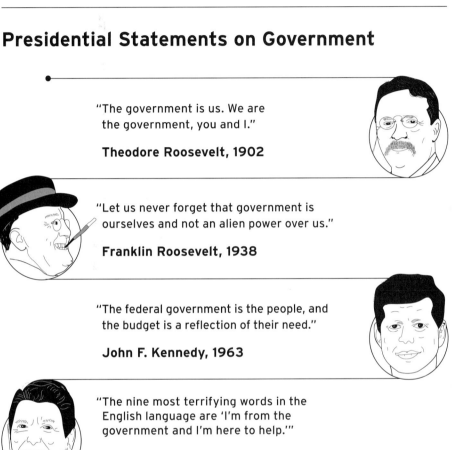

"The government is us. We are the government, you and I."

Theodore Roosevelt, 1902

"Let us never forget that government is ourselves and not an alien power over us."

Franklin Roosevelt, 1938

"The federal government is the people, and the budget is a reflection of their need."

John F. Kennedy, 1963

"The nine most terrifying words in the English language are 'I'm from the government and I'm here to help.'"

Ronald Reagan, 1986

"The era of big government is over.... Our federal government today is the smallest it has been in 30 years, and it's getting smaller every day."

Bill Clinton, 1996

Declining Infrastructure

In 1966, the U.S. committed 2.5% of its potential GDP to infrastructure investment—roads, bridges, schools, hospitals, water treatment, sewers, and more. Over the next twenty years, mainly during the Nixon and Reagan administrations, infrastructure investment fell dramatically, hitting a record low of 1.3% of GDP in 1983, and it's held at a relatively steady state ever since. And that understates the underinvestment, as construction material prices have outpaced inflation in recent years.

In practical terms, what does this mean? Simple: worse conditions for working Americans. About 1 in every 5 U.S. roads is in poor condition. Forty-five percent of Americans do not have access to public transit. A water main break occurs every two minutes. Numerous faults in our core infrastructure have led to crises that once seemed unimaginable: In Flint, Michigan, 12,000 children drank lead-contaminated water, causing irreparable brain damage that affects academic performance and IQ and increases the likelihood of Alzheimer's and Legionnaires' disease. In Miami a twelve-story beachfront condominium collapsed, killing 98 people.

Meanwhile, as a share of GDP, China spends ten times more on infrastructure than the U.S. Which may explain why it takes 4.5 hours to take a train from Shanghai to Beijing (752 miles) but 7 hours to get from Boston to D.C. (438 miles).

03

Infrastructure Spending as Share of Potential GDP

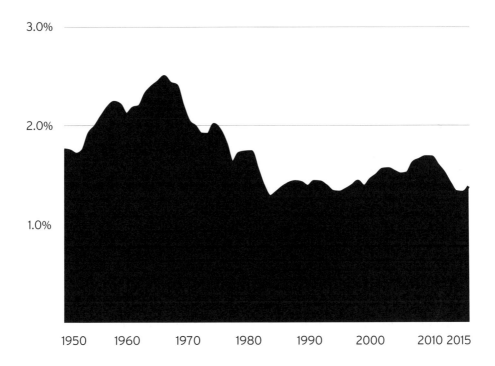

Sources: Economic Policy Institute, Bureau of Economic Analysis, Congressional Budget Office.

Note: Includes public investment in hospital and educational structures, highways, sewers, transportation facilities, and conservation and development.

Healthcare Cutbacks

The pruning of the U.S. social safety net had many facets. Unemployment and welfare benefits were cut back, urban infrastructure spending was reduced, and federal funding and oversight was decreased in favor of community control. One change with profound, long-term effects on our communities was cutting public mental healthcare. In the 1960s and '70s, a national movement to "deinstitutionalize" mental health patients drastically reduced the availability of psychiatric care. For many, this was a blessing, but hundreds of thousands of people with serious mental health issues were left to fend for themselves.

The implications of this shift were widely recognized, but the nation was losing its will to protect the vulnerable. In 1963, President Kennedy advanced legislation to establish a federal system of mental health treatment, but after his assasination funding was unreliable and the system never thrived. President Carter attempted to renew Kennedy's vision, but Reagan, who supported deinstitutionalization as governor of California, gutted Carter's program.

Today, more than half a million Americans are homeless every night. Twenty percent of them suffer from a severe mental illness, and 17% from chronic substance abuse. Studies have found a direct correlation between decreases in psychiatric hospital beds and rising homelessness. Mentally ill people are three times more likely to be the victim of a crime; they frequently become the burden of law enforcement and the prison system when their illness goes untreated. This national problem has been left at the feet of local governments.

04

Number of Psychiatric Inpatient Beds

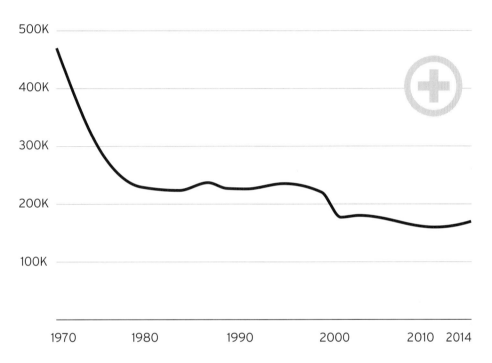

Source: National Association of State Mental Health Program Directors.

Labor Loses Its Voice

In 1950, nearly 1 in 3 American non-farm workers was represented by a union, which gave them the ability to organize and exercise bargaining power against powerful employers. And exercise power they did: That year, the U.S. experienced 424 strikes involving more than 1,000 workers. But labor actions declined dramatically beginning in 1980, and by 1988 there were just 40 such stoppages.

Labor actions improved working conditions and wages, but the union movement didn't fade away on account of its success: Unfair labor practice charges remained well above the historical average through the 1980s. A range of factors caused the decline in union power—including corruption and overreaching by unions themselves—but the result was a power shift ... from labor to capital.

05

Worker Strikes and Unfair Labor Practice Charges

■ Worker strikes   — **Unfair labor practice charges**

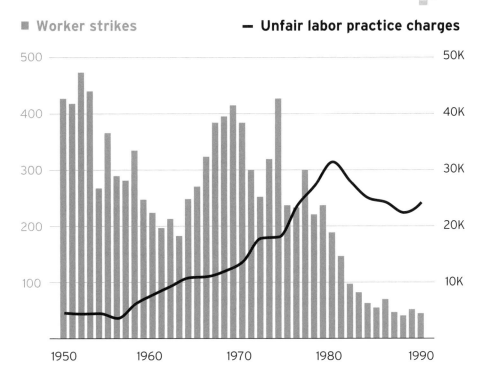

Sources: Bureau of Labor Statistics, National Labor Review Board, Economic Policy Institute.

Note: Strikes involving 1,000 or more workers.

The LBO Boom

In 1982, Gibson Greeting Cards was purchased for $80 million, of which only $1 million was contributed by the acquiring investor—the rest was borrowed. Back then, the notion of financing an acquisition almost entirely with debt was strange. But after Gibson IPO'd at $290 million and the investor made off with $66 million in cash, the strategy caught on like wildfire, ushering in the leveraged buyout (LBO) boom. "It's kind of frightening to make this kind of money," said the greeting card tycoon, former treasury secretary William Simon.

Within seven years, leveraged buyouts went from making up 1% of mergers and acquisitions (M&As) in America to 30%. Corporate raiders were the inquisition of the new religion. Any management team that wasn't maximizing shareholder returns got bounced, and their company sold for parts to finance the debt. This led to the bankruptcy of many acquired companies. By the time the trend had cooled off in the early '90s, the LBO industry's pockets were more than stuffed.

06

Leveraged Buyout Volume as Percentage of M&A Volume

■ Leveraged buyout volume

Source: Piper Sandler.

Note: Domestic deals only.

Productivity Soars, Compensation Stagnates

Productivity is an economic measure of efficiency: the ratio of output to input. U.S. productivity has increased at a remarkably steady rate since the 1950s, meaning we keep getting better at getting more value out of our labor, equipment, and raw materials. From 1950 to the mid-'70s, average compensation kept pace with productivity, meaning the benefits of productivity gains went to those doing the work.

Since then, productivity and wages have decoupled. The value of our output has kept climbing, but the compensation of our workers has stopped reflecting it. Between 1973 and 2014, net productivity grew 72%, but hourly worker compensation grew just 9%. This left worker compensation at less than half what it would have been if the two had stayed in line. In other words, our nation kept winning, but our workers only got to cash in half their chips. The money started going somewhere else.

07

Productivity Relative to Hourly Compensation

Indexed to 1948

— **Productivity**   — **Hourly compensation**

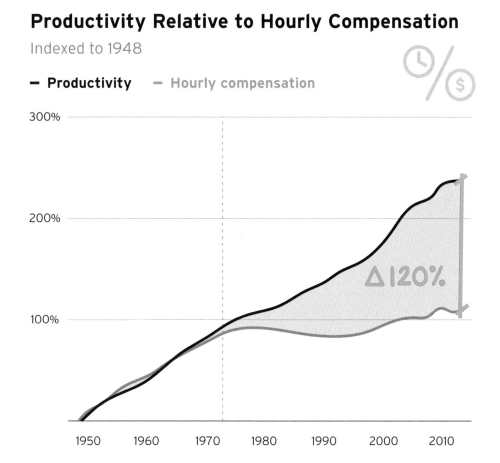

Sources: Bureau of Economic Analysis, Bureau of Labor Statistics, Economic Policy Institute.

Note: Productivity equals net output for U.S. goods and services minus depreciation, per hour worked. Hourly compensation is inflation-adjusted and accounts for U.S. non-management workers.

Income Inequality

Since the 1970s, the nation has evolved from a manufacturing economy to an information economy. The highly educated reaped the benefits of this shift; between 1979 and 2013, the top 1% of American earners saw their wages increase almost 140%. That cohort, largely made up of executives, lawyers, and physicians, has become significantly more populated with ... bankers. In 1979, 8 in 100 members of the 1% worked in finance. By 2005, that number had nearly doubled to 14.

While the elites ran, the rest of our nation crawled. The bottom 99% of Americans experienced wage growth that was nearly eight times slower than that of the top 1%, making it significantly harder to build wealth and almost impossible to enjoy the upward mobility their parents had.

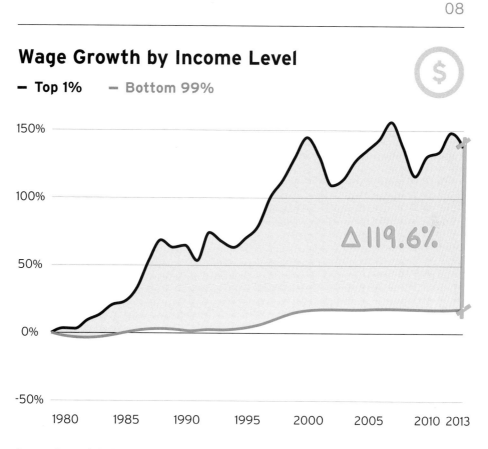

08

Wage Growth by Income Level

— **Top 1%**   — Bottom 99%

△ 119.6%

Sources: Economic Policy Institute; Kopczuk, Saez, and Song.

An Overwhelmed IRS

In 1960, the Internal Revenue Service audited more than 3% of America's tax returns to make sure individuals and corporations were paying their fair share. That number has fallen dramatically, to less than 0.5%. At the same time, six decades of tax "reform" has expanded the maze of loopholes and the potential for fraud and error.

It's estimated that we lose roughly $600 billion in unpaid taxes every year, with the wealthiest 1% responsible for 28% of that number.

09

IRS Audit Rates

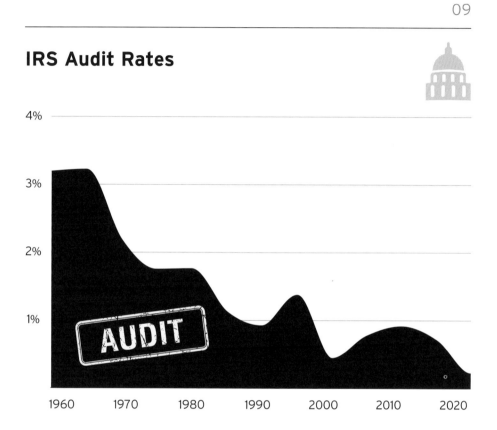

Source: Internal Revenue Service.

Note: Inclusive of all tax return categories.

The Offshoring Explosion

A complex tax code gives a competitive advantage to large corporations, which have the resources to exploit it. One favored tactic is offshoring profits—setting up shell companies in countries that have lower corporate tax rates or offer incentives, such as Bermuda, Ireland, Singapore, and Switzerland.

In 1966, roughly 5% of corporate profits were booked in tax havens abroad. But corporations soon realized the easiest way to increase shareholder value was to not pay taxes, and by 2000 well over a quarter of their profits were registered in tax havens. By 2016, that share had increased to more than half.

10

Share of U.S. Multinational Corporate Profits Booked in Foreign Tax Havens

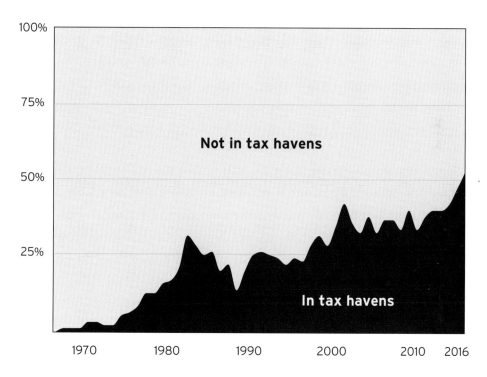

Source: National Bureau of Economic Research.

Note: Includes all non-oil sectors.

Stock Market Participation

For the past twenty-five years, roughly half of American households
have had a personal stake in the stock market thanks to 401(k)
retirement accounts, mutual funds, and the internet, which turned
business news and investment media into a Main Street product and
rendered the market our primary economic indicator. In 1989, less than
a third of U.S. households had any holdings—direct or indirect—in the
stock market. By 2019 that share had increased to roughly half.

This was an improvement, but it did little to slow the runaway train that
is wealth inequality. The fact remains that nearly half of American
households don't have any stake in the stock market. Furthermore,
the distribution of stock is enormously uneven. The wealthiest 1% of
Americans hold almost half the stocks owned by households. The bottom
80% hold just 13%.

11

Share of U.S. Households Invested in the Stock Market

Direct and indirect holdings

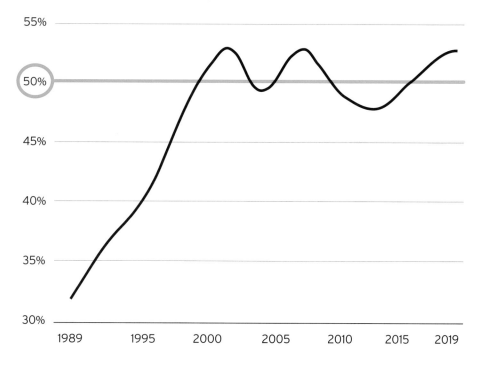

Sources: Federal Reserve, Survey of Consumer Finances.

CHAPTER 2

The World We Made

*Unshackled capitalism proved to be
a potent force for economic productivity,
globalization, and democratization.*

The ascent of the American economy after World War II, coupled with the advances of technology, brought unprecedented prosperity not just to the U.S., but to the human race. It's tempting to let the costs of that prosperity obscure it, but a sober accounting of America and the world today would be incomplete without recognizing our enormous gains.

The world is significantly wealthier, freer, healthier, and better educated than it was forty years ago. In 1980, over 40% of humanity lived in extreme poverty. Today, less than 10% does. In 1980, 44% of humanity had no democratic rights. Today, it is less than 25%. A child born in 1980 had a life expectancy of 63 years. A child born today should live a decade longer. In 1980, 30% of people fifteen years and older had no formal education. By 2015, that share had been cut in half.

These were global gains, but America lay at the heart of them. U.S. innovation in everything from transport to advertising supercharged the consumer culture of the postwar era into an upward dance between demand and manufacturing agility.

The billions lifted from poverty since 1980 were largely in Asia, and their means of ascent was making consumer goods for U.S. and European markets. Those same economies are today converting to knowledge work and middle-class lifestyles, in substantial part on the foundation of digital technologies developed in the former orange groves of the Bay Area.

We tend to focus on things that did occur, but we shouldn't overlook crises that were averted. The demise of the Soviet Union posed an apocalyptic risk. By 1989, the Soviets commanded 39,000 nuclear warheads and the world's largest standing army. Managing the sudden collapse of one of history's largest empires could have gone very, very badly. At one point, the Soviet government sold twenty naval combat ships for cases of Pepsi. But postwar institutions crafted and nurtured by the Western nations held firm.

For better or worse (it's both), the headline change is increased global connectivity. The term "globalization" has been loaded up with the anxieties of our era, but it represents a profound change in the human condition beyond the concerns of the moment. Never before has human knowledge been so widespread, nor have creators, from artists to manufacturers, had access to such a breadth of markets—and competitors.

Productivity Revolution

Modern civilization rests on a foundation of unprecedented, once even unimaginable productivity. The rebuilding of Western Europe and the conversion of the U.S. wartime economy after World War II doubled the globe's annual economic output in less than a decade. By 1960, the world was producing twenty times as much as it had in the early nineteenth century.

Then, as the relatively easy gains from the postwar boom wound down, the real miracle happened. From 1980 to 2004, the world's economic output doubled again, from $35 trillion to $70 trillion. In just twenty-four years, a single generation, as much economic potency had come online as had taken the human species its entire history to accumulate. Today, the world generates roughly as much output in a month as it did in the entire year of 1950.

12

Global GDP Growth

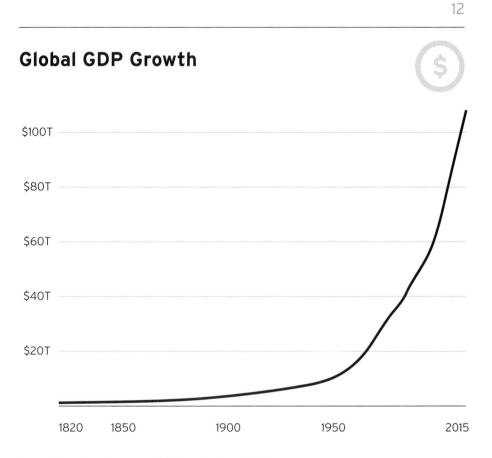

Source: World Bank & Maddison (2017) via Our World in Data.

Billions of People Work Their Way Out of Poverty

In less than forty years, billions of people have improved their lot and made it out of extreme poverty. That's a low bar—$1.90 per day, which is subsistence living even in low-cost economies—but it's still a change for the better unlike anything in history.

The rolling back of poverty has been particularly remarkable in China. In 1990, 750 million Chinese lived below the international poverty line. Today, it's less than 10 million. Most of these people still have low incomes, but the economic engine they're a part of continues to churn. In 2019, there were 100 million households in China with wealth of more than $110,000.

The modern world order has ample flaws, but sometimes the scale of our achievement is so vast, we lose sight of it.

13

Percentage of Population Living in Households Below the Global Poverty Line

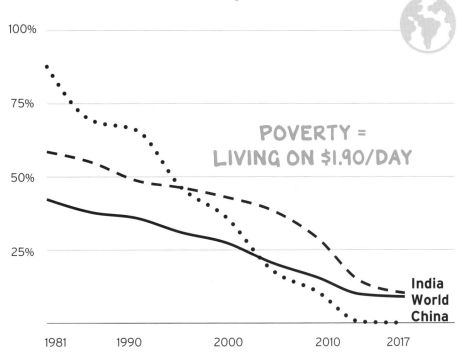

POVERTY = LIVING ON $1.90/DAY

India
World
China

Source: PovcalNet (World Bank).

Health Is Wealth

Thanks to substantial improvements in healthcare, sanitation, education, and economic opportunity, people all over the world are living longer. Infant mortality has been cut by two-thirds since 1990; disease and war take fewer lives. This is the ultimate measure of prosperity and human accomplishment: more life.

14

Increases in Life Expectancy

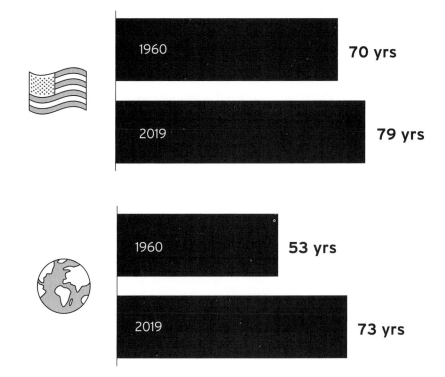

Source: World Bank.

A New World Order

Democracy has long been the backbone of America's prosperity and the reason for its progress on the world stage—and we have much of the post–World War II era to thank for that. While the rise of democracy ticked up steadily from the 1940s through the '70s, it wasn't until 1980 that a real shift away from autocracy took hold. The change came with the end of the Cold War, when autocratic regimes fell apart due to dwindling economic and political backing.

No other form of sovereignty gives power to people the way democracy does. It sits on a bed of legitimacy, justice, freedom. It promotes innovation, prosperity, and healthy governance. As we battle misinformation and political divisiveness, maintaining our democracy is vital to the health and wealth of not only this country but also those that turn to us for leadership on the world stage.

15

The Number of Countries Under Autocracies vs. Democracies

Autocracies	Democracies

Source: Varieties of Democracy Project (2019, version 9).

Freedom of Movement

I've long admired the work of immigrants. I like to humblebrag that I was raised by a single immigrant mother and that both she and my father came to America with nothing. Without their courage and desire—the dose of selfishness that drove them to migrate here and seek a better life—I would be nowhere near where I am today.

Immigrating is hard and risky, and it usually means something went wrong at the point of embarkation. But increasing migration also means our world is more connected and more people have access to opportunities and success. Migrants contribute to technological and scientific advancements, to business innovation, and to a more robust labor force. Between 1990 and 2005, immigrants started a quarter of all venture-backed public companies in the U.S. In 2018, immigrants founded or cofounded more than half of America's "unicorns" (private companies valued at more than one billion U.S. dollars), and as of 2020, immigrants to the U.S. were starting businesses at nearly double the rate of people born here.

16

Percent Increase of Migrants
Every Five Years

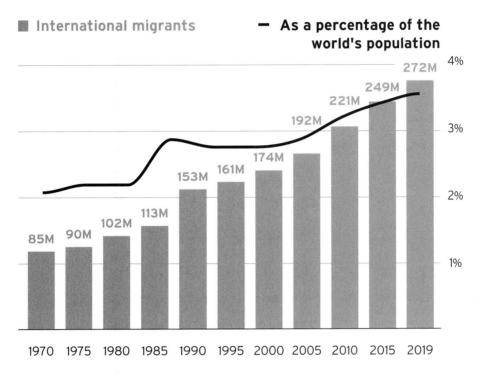

▪ International migrants   — **As a percentage of the
world's population**

Source: IOM World Migration Report 2020.

The Red Blood Cells of the Consumer Economy

The shipping container is one of the most transformative design innovations of the twentieth century. An engineer named Keith Tantlinger made this revolutionary mode of transport possible in the mid-1950s when he created a way to stack containers on top of one another, for efficient shipment and rapid loading and unloading by crane. Not only was Tatlinger's design cheap and easy to build, its standardization allowed containers to be imported and exported seamlessly across nations and shipping lines.

Our obsession with stuff and consumerism—made possible by these stacked metal boxes—is not going away. Between 1980 and 2017, the number of goods carried by shipping containers increased from 102 million metric tons to about 1.83 billion metric tons, and it's estimated that 80% of all goods are now carried by sea.

17

Capacity of Container Ships in Seaborne Trade

In dead weight tonnage

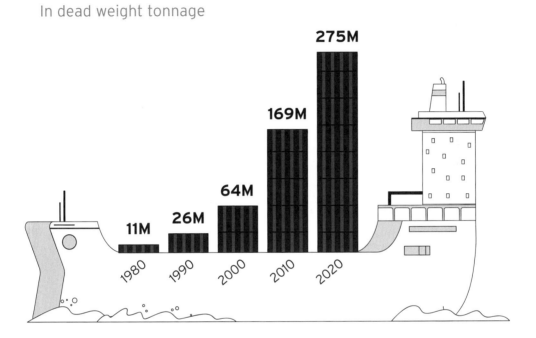

Sources: UISL; Marine Flottenkommando via Statista.

The Digital Age

In a world where the internet is the bridge to opportunity, communication, information, and the economy, it's a relief that since 2005, we've seen a 206% increase in the number of people accessing this lifeline. Think about it: People rely on Google search results more than any other entity in history. The internet may serve as a breeding ground for misinformation, ransom-seeking criminals, and the darkest corners of humanity, but most of what we enjoy today wouldn't be possible without it.

The way we shop, dine, date, learn, work, navigate, and entertain ourselves has all been morphed—for better or worse—by our ability to connect online. Had it not been for the web, our connection to society would've shuttered along with our beloved storefronts and restaurants during the Covid-19 pandemic.

It was estimated that every minute in 2020, transactions worth nearly $240,000 were made on Venmo, 41.6 million messages were sent on WhatsApp, more than 400,000 hours of video were streamed on Netflix, at least 2,700 people installed TikTok, and 6,600 packages got shipped by Amazon.

18

Global Access to the Internet

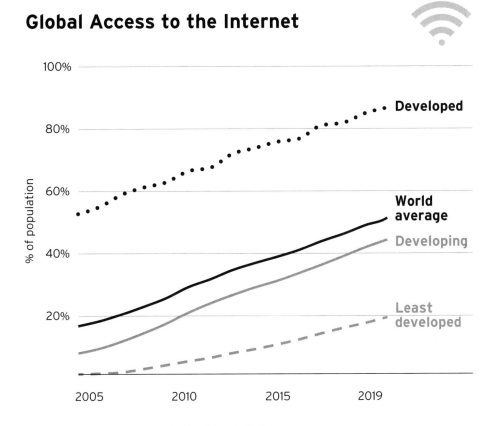

Source: International Telecommunication Union via Statista.

Accelerating Technological Advancement

Two "laws" help explain the extraordinary changes wrought by the global adoption of the internet. The first is Moore's Law, named for Gordon Moore, an Intel cofounder. In the 1960s, he observed that the number of transistors that could be squeezed into a single chip was increasing at a predictable rate—doubling about every eighteen months. Thanks to billions of dollars in R&D and engineering investment, that rate of improvement has held ever since.

The second law is named after Bob Metcalfe, the inventor of Ethernet, one of the protocols foundational to the internet. Metcalfe posited that the value of a network is equal to the number of connections *between* users, not just the number of users. Bigger is better, and better, and better.

These laws help us quantify something we can see in our online experience: both the power of our devices and the value of the network they're attached to are millions of times greater than they were at the dawn of the internet era. Plotting this growth reveals an interesting twist, however. For the past thirty years, the value of the internet as described by Metcalfe's Law has increased more than processing power has improved. But as internet penetration slows, so does the rate of increase in the value of the internet. Meanwhile, Moore's Law chugs along, suggesting that we may be approaching an inflection point, when changes to our online experience are driven more by technological advancement than by the ever-growing number of online connections.

19

Moore's and Metcalfe's Laws

Indexed, 1990 = 1 (log scale)

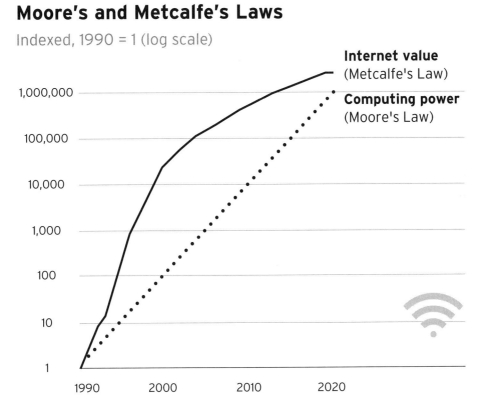

Internet value
(Metcalfe's Law)

Computing power
(Moore's Law)

Sources: World Bank, Prof G analysis.

U.S. Institutions = Genius Factories

Nobel prizes have been given since 1901 in physics, chemistry, medicine, literature, and peace. The prize is awarded to "those who, during the preceding year, shall have conferred the greatest benefit to humankind." Nearly half of the science and economics prizes have gone to luminaries associated with U.S. institutions—which speaks much to the strength of those institutions. One more thing ... more than a third of U.S.-affiliated Nobel laureates in the past decade have been immigrants.

20

***

Research Affiliations of Nobel Laureates

Physics, chemistry, physiology, medicine, and economic sciences

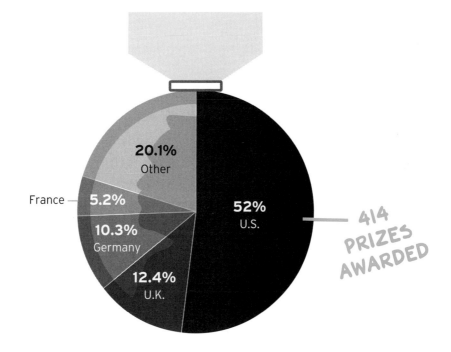

France —

Source: Nobel Prize Outreach.

Assisting Humanity

The postwar U.S. did not invest solely in its domestic recovery; it made multibillion-dollar investments in its weakened allies and fallen foes alike, including the $13.3 billion Marshall Plan. That tradition has continued: the U.S. remains the world's largest provider of foreign aid (although it's not the most generous on a share-of-GDP basis).

Since 1980, the U.S. has extended roughly $1 trillion in nonmilitary aid, typically on a bipartisan basis. President Reagan directed over $1 billion in direct response to famine in Africa, and urged Congress to substantially increase foreign aid funding. President George W. Bush made game-changing commitments to programs fighting HIV/AIDS, famine, and corruption in Africa. President Obama's Feed the Future program invested in global food security, a program reauthorized under President Trump in 2018. U.S. private foundations, meanwhile, provide over half the world's philanthropic expenditures.

Some say we should have more businesspeople in government. I admire great business leaders, but government is not business. Business teaches us to always look for an advantage, to not give anything away without getting more in return. That's the antithesis of government (and government service), the purpose of which is to contribute to the commonwealth without recompense.

21

Cumulative U.S. Foreign Aid Nonmilitary Expenditure

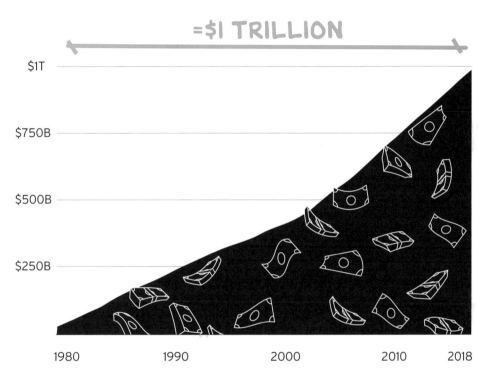

=$1 TRILLION

$1T

$750B

$500B

$250B

1980   1990   2000   2010   2018

Source: ForeignAssistance.gov.

CHAPTER 3

Idolatry of Innovators

*We put our faith in technology and lionize
the entrepreneurs who have best exploited it.*

The Reagan Revolution celebrated the individual. And while the "average Joe" was an effective political prop, the narrative required a heroic leader. So as the tide of economic prosperity lifted most boats, in America we increasingly transferred credit for the rise from the laboring masses to the brilliant, opportunistic, or just lucky individuals directing those masses. The void created by a decrease in church attendance and reliance on a superbeing was filled by a modern-day savior: the innovator.

Individualism is embedded in the American story. We celebrate the cowboys who (supposedly) tamed the West, and we revere the inventors and industrialists who (ostensibly) built the country's commercial might. This idolatry of innovators is most deeply embedded in the culture of technology. It's an article of faith in tech that success is the result of individual achievement, a mark of grit and genius.

For much of my adult life, this was my own mythology of self, that I'd gone from being the child of a single, working mother to shopping for private jets. *Clearly* I was self-made. But the truth is that I'm American-made. I benefited from being born in a time and place of unprecedented prosperity with a host of advantages, most of them circumstantial. Endemic to tech culture is the conflation of luck and talent.

There is a unique ecosystem in Silicon Valley, and the human capital it attracts is inspiring. What gets less attention is that the foundation of the Valley was built on government projects. The computer chip, the internet, the mouse, the web browser, and

GPS were all midwifed with tax dollars. While the conversion of those technologies into private profits took individual vision, it also took millions of hours of work from thousands of engineers and other wage earners, most of whom were the product of one of the largest government programs we have: public schools.

Similarly, while technologies are neither heroes nor saints, we get seduced by their capabilities and blinded to the risks they present. I published my first book, *The Four*, in 2017. It began as a love letter to technology and the achievements of the internet era. But the more I studied the companies and people behind all that innovation, the more alarmed I became by their power and reach. At the time, it was a hard sell. Not many people wanted to hear that their new God, Big Tech, might not be concerned with the condition of our souls or take care of us when we're older. The risks of tech obsession are clearer now.

The nation once idolized astronauts and civil rights leaders who inspired hope and empathy. Now it worships tech innovators who generate billions and move financial markets. We get the heroes we deserve.

Turning Away From Community Organizations

We used to be more involved in our communities. In the 1990s, most Americans attended some form of religious service, and large numbers got involved in community-based clubs like Rotary and enrolled their kids in team-building programs like the Boy Scouts and Girl Scouts. But over the course of the past thirty years, something's changed. Now fewer than half of Americans go to a church, temple, or mosque, and many of us no longer talk to our neighbors. Our commitment to our communities has lagged, and the number of Rotary members and kids enrolled in scouting programs dwindles every year.

It's likely that some of the engagement we once found in these forums has moved online. But Facebook is no substitute for face-to-face conversations or the deep connections we form working alongside others for the betterment of the community. Studies of our interactions show that real-world interactions with others increase empathy and tolerance generally. Researchers in the U.K. found that residential segregation led to decreased tolerance of minority residents, while residential integration led to improved relationships between groups. The inevitable question is: What degree of tolerance will we lose when we stop engaging with and integrating into our communities?

22

Decline in Community-Based Activities in the U.S.

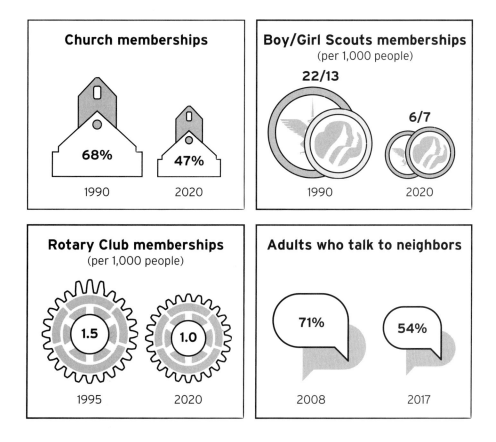

Church memberships	**Boy/Girl Scouts memberships** (per 1,000 people)
68% — 1990 / 47% — 2020	22/13 — 1990 / 6/7 — 2020
Rotary Club memberships (per 1,000 people)	**Adults who talk to neighbors**
1.5 — 1995 / 1.0 — 2020	71% — 2008 / 54% — 2017

Sources: Analysis of data from Gallup, Senate.gov, U.S. Census via AllCountries, AP News, Baraboo News Republic, and Word on the Street.

Water Safety in the Richest Country in the World

In 2019, EPA administrator Andrew Wheeler bragged that in the U.S., 92% of all drinking water met safety standards. What Wheeler could have said is that 8% of the water in America is not safe to drink. If 8% of Americans drank that water, 26 million people would be at risk.

To put that number in perspective, 97% of American adults have a cell phone. Tech companies have found a way to put a supercomputer in our pockets, yet the U.S. government cannot ensure safe drinking water for our entire population.

23

American Adults Who Own a Cell Phone vs. Share of Drinking Water in the U.S. That Meets EPA Standards

Cell phone statistics from 2021, clean water from 2019

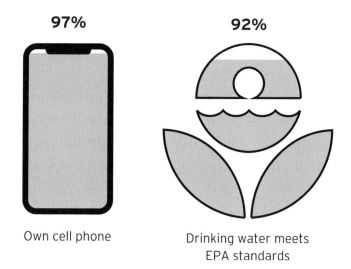

97%

Own cell phone

92%

Drinking water meets
EPA standards

Sources: Pew Research Center, EPA Administrator Andrew Wheeler
via *CBS News* interview.

Privatized R&D = Privatized Progress

The payout horizon for research and development is often distant, but those payouts can be enormous. In the 1950s and '60s, federal government investment in emerging digital technologies laid the foundation for the unprecedented tech boom of the past forty years. Consider the iPhone: all of its core technologies flow from those public sector investments, from the chip at its heart to the GPS satellites and the global network on which it depends.

Federal funding for R&D as a share of GDP has declined steadily since that golden era, from a peak of 1.9% to 0.7% in 2019. Private investment has filled the breach—total R&D spend as a percentage of GDP is slightly higher today than it was in the '60s. But leaving the future up to private interests is shortsighted.

First, private investments are subject to short-term market pressures, and as virtuous as the discipline of making your quarterly numbers can be, it's too limiting for the long-term, uncharted inquiry of deep R&D. Second, because private investment means private ownership, the fruits of this research won't be fully exploited by nor subject to the democratic controls of government management.

The R&D labs of today are pushing the boundaries of artificial intelligence, genetic manipulation, and viral replication. Do we want those technologies in the hands of elected officials, or under the exclusive control of Elon and Zuck?

24

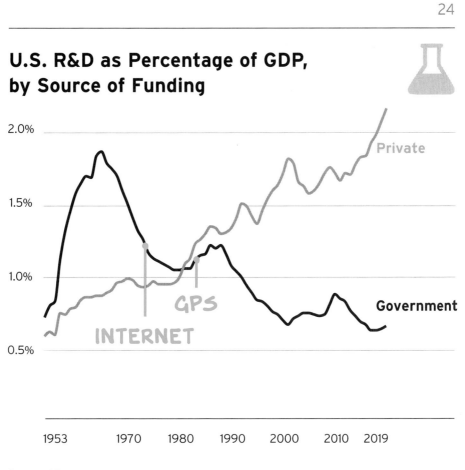

U.S. R&D as Percentage of GDP, by Source of Funding

2.0%

Private

1.5%

1.0%

GPS

INTERNET

Government

0.5%

1953 1970 1980 1990 2000 2010 2019

Source: NSF.

College Has Become the Entry Requirement to the Middle Class

More jobs require postsecondary education and training beyond high school now than ever before. At the same time, college degrees are more expensive and exclusive than they've ever been. The convergence of these trends has intensified inequality among those who are lucky enough to obtain a degree and those who aren't.

While access to college has improved for women and people of color, and more people as a whole are attending college today than did in the '70s, acceptance rates across the board have declined markedly and prices have skyrocketed. Meanwhile, lower-skilled jobs have been sent overseas and repetitive tasks left to computers. Increasingly, available jobs are complex and require a postsecondary education.

What to do? I'm an advocate of increasing enrollment drastically at America's public universities by adopting hybrid models of instruction. But we also need more options for vocational training, such that non-college-bound youth can learn important trades that will allow them to create financial security.

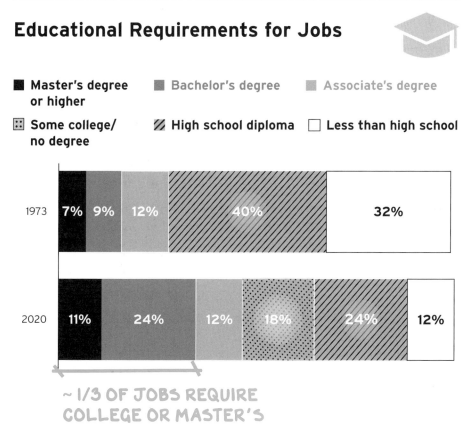

25

Educational Requirements for Jobs

■ Master's degree or higher   ■ Bachelor's degree   ■ Associate's degree

▦ Some college/ no degree   ▨ High school diploma   □ Less than high school

1973: 7% | 9% | 12% | 40% | 32%

2020: 11% | 24% | 12% | 18% | 24% | 12%

~1/3 OF JOBS REQUIRE COLLEGE OR MASTER'S

Source: Georgetown Center for Education and the Workforce.

Note: Decimals rounded to whole percentages.

The Gross Idolatry of Innovators ... by Innovators

When Apple filed to become a public company in 1980, "Steve Jobs" showed up in the S-1 paperwork (the form a company files with the SEC before going public) eight times. When Microsoft filed its prospectus in 1986, "Bill Gates" appeared twenty-three times. Jobs and Gates were both visionary founders and leaders who were already making the future, and were dominant figures at the companies they had founded.

Then there's Adam Neumann. When his company WeWork filed to go public in 2019, "Adam" appeared 169 times in its prospectus. Many of those references described the complex self-dealing transactions he'd concocted to extract as much wealth as possible from investors. About a month after the S-1 filing, the IPO was canceled and Neumann was fired.

Neumann's an extreme example, but the idolatry of innovators is all over recent IPO filings. The name of Affirm's cofounder and CEO, Max Levchin, shows up 131 times in its S-1, and Robinhood's cofounder and CEO, Vladimir Tenev, appears 109 times.

Our educational institutions, and an abundance of VC capital, are making it possible to succeed, wildly. In America, it's never been easier to become a billionaire—but it's never been harder to become a millionaire.

26

Number of Mentions of Founder in S-1 Filings

169
Adam Neumann
WeWork, 2019

131
Max Levchin
Affirm, 2021

109
Vladimir Tenev
Robinhood, 2021

23
Bill Gates
Microsoft, 1986

8
Steve Jobs
Apple, 1980

Source: Prof G analysis of S-1 filings.

Power Games

Until very recently, going public implied the transition of a company from a benevolent dictatorship to a republic, where ownership is distributed and decision-making power lies in an elected body (the board). This is increasingly not the case in tech. Company insiders, usually the founders and leading venture capitalists, are securing unprecedented control of the public companies that employ them.

The key to securing this control is the dual-class share structure. In a regular company's stock structure, each share equals one vote. In a dual-class structure, certain shares have more voting power than others. These privileged shares are reserved exclusively for company insiders, giving them control over the company's operations and insulating them from outside shareholder pressure.

In December 2019, I took a small stake in Twitter and wrote a public letter to the board, highlighting the company's lack of innovation and weak shareholder returns, and calling on them to replace part-time CEO Jack Dorsey. A few months later, Elliott Management, a large activist fund, called me and said they were signing my letter with a $2 billion pen and secured three seats on Twitter's board of directors. Less than two years later, Dorsey "resigned." (Read: He was fired with dignity.) It's unlikely Elliott would have been able to make this change—which will benefit shareholders—if Twitter had two classes of shares. Now, 46% of tech companies go public with a dual-class structure.

27

Share of Tech IPOs With Dual-Class Structures

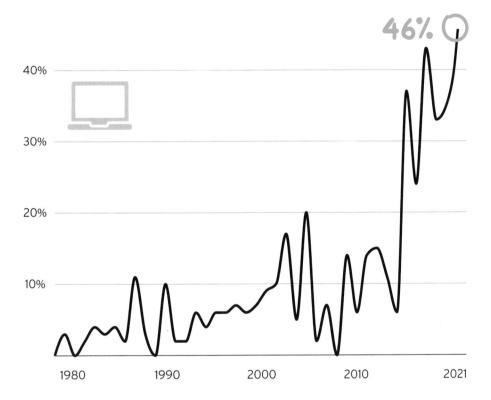

Sources: Jay R. Ritter, Warrington College of Business, University of Florida.

The Entrenchment of Wealth

Owning stock, as opposed to strictly dollar bills, is one of the most foolproof ways to grow one's wealth in America. And the good news is that U.S. households own around half of the $50 trillion U.S. stock market. But the distribution of that wealth is grossly unequal. Eighty-nine percent of that stock is owned by the wealthiest 10% of households, an outsized share that's been getting larger over time. (In 1990, it was 82%.)

How have the wealthiest Americans entrenched themselves? It's because of policies that favor the already wealthy while diminishing opportunities for the lower and middle classes.

Consider the tax code: income gained from selling stock in a company is taxed at a lower rate than income gained from actually working at that business. A second transfer from poor to rich: a homeowner may deduct mortgage interest on a first and second home, while the less wealthy pay nondeductible rent. We've functionally decided money (and the money it makes) is more noble than sweat.

These transfers are pitched to the American public as how to get wealthy, when in reality, they describe how to stay wealthy. The messaging is propaganda brought to you by the 10% of people who own 89% of the stocks.

28

Stock Ownership in the U.S. by Wealth

2021

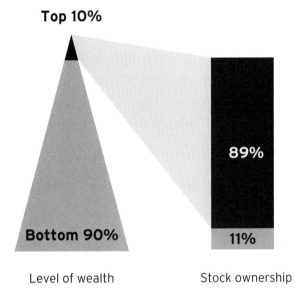

Top 10%

Bottom 90%

89%

11%

Level of wealth   Stock ownership

Source: Federal Reserve Bank of St. Louis.

It's Never Been Easier to Be a Trillion-Dollar Company

In August 2018, Apple became the first public company to reach a $1 trillion valuation. At the time, its annual revenue was $229 billion. In October 2021, Tesla became the sixth company to reach $1 trillion, with each company reaching that mark on less revenue than the company before it. Tesla arrived in the four-comma club with a mere $32 billion in revenue.

Stock valuations used to be about fundamentals and technicals. Now they're about storytelling and the vision the CEO concocts and the media propagates. The result? Shares in virtually bankrupt companies like AMC and Hertz spiked 1,000% in 2021, and three electric-vehicle firms—Tesla, Lucid, and Rivian—were together worth more than the auto and airline industries combined.

The trend continues: It took Apple forty-two years to be worth $1 trillion in 2018, two years to hit $2 trillion, and seventeen months to hit $3 trillion.

29

Revenue the Year Before Trillion-Dollar Valuation

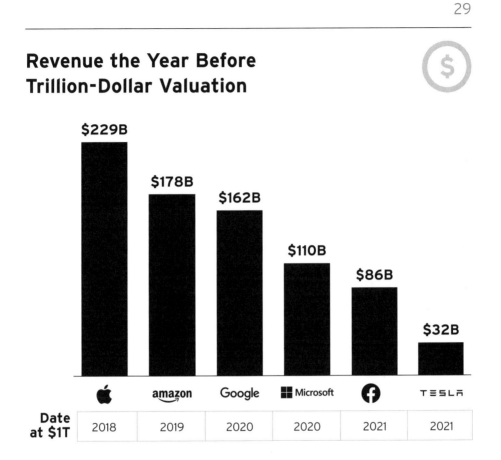

| $229B | $178B | $162B | $110B | $86B | $32B |

Date at $1T	2018	2019	2020	2020	2021	2021

Sources: George Maroudas via Twitter, Prof G analysis.

The MDMA Dealer of Capitalism Is the Corporate Communications Exec

There's an inverse correlation between the level of bullshit in a company's mission statement and its actual performance.

More specifically, companies have fallen in love with "yogababble," a term I coined a few years ago to describe the nonsensical pontification that had replaced English in tech unicorns' mission statements. At best, a company mission statement describes the purpose and value of its product in a clear, concise manner. At worst, it massively exaggerates the cosmic relevance of a business, totally obscuring its actual product and means of generating revenue. At worst, a mission statement is yogababble.

Yogababble grew up in the brand era, when inanimate objects started to take on animate characteristics. Objects and companies could be personified—likable, young, cool, patriotic. Corporate comms execs began to scale the charisma and vision of their business's founder. Overpromise and underdeliver became a means for access to cheap capital. (Elon Musk, April 2019: "A year from now, we'll have over a million cars with full self-driving." Number of such cars on the road in early 2022: zero.) The lines between charm, vision, bullshit, and fraud have nearly evaporated. The smokescreen that enables this kind of bad party trick is yogababble.

30

Yogababble

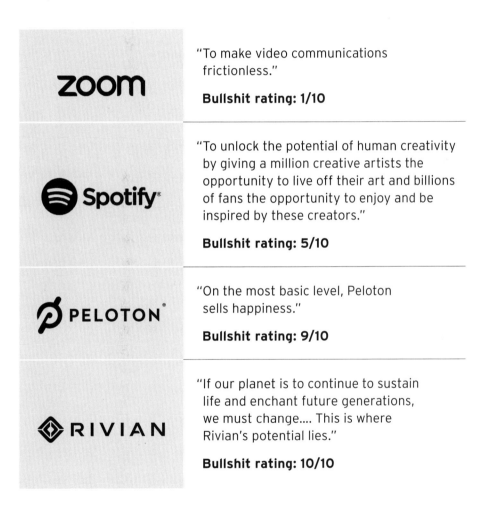

"To make video communications frictionless."

Bullshit rating: 1/10

"To unlock the potential of human creativity by giving a million creative artists the opportunity to live off their art and billions of fans the opportunity to enjoy and be inspired by these creators."

Bullshit rating: 5/10

"On the most basic level, Peloton sells happiness."

Bullshit rating: 9/10

"If our planet is to continue to sustain life and enchant future generations, we must change…. This is where Rivian's potential lies."

Bullshit rating: 10/10

Source: Prof G analysis.

D.C. = HQ2

Spending on lobbying by U.S. tech firms has ballooned by more than eleven times in the past twenty years. In 2000, tech companies spent $7 million courting legislators. Twenty years later, they spent $80 million—more than the commercial banking industry ($62 million) and approaching the budget of oil and gas ($113 million). Facebook spent $20 million on lobbying in 2020, followed closely by Amazon with $19 million and Alphabet (Google's parent company) with $8 million.

And that's just in formal lobbying budgets. Jeff Bezos owns *The Washington Post* (conveniently, the biggest media company in D.C.), and he's building Amazon's second headquarters (HQ2) across the river from—shocker!—the capital city. Uber, Lyft, and their gig-economy peers spent over $200 million to promote Proposition 22 in California, which protected transportation and delivery app companies from the obligation to offer healthcare and other benefits to their drivers.

31

Lobbying Spend by the U.S. Tech Sector

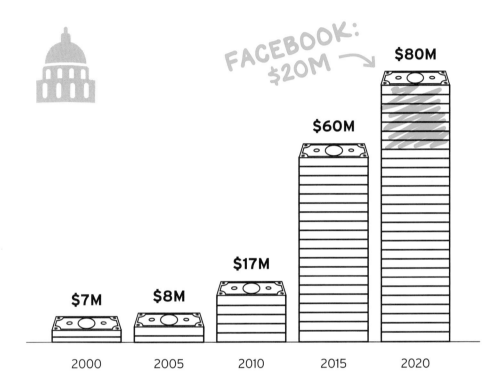

Source: OpenSecrets.

Perspective

Morning shows in America spent almost as much time talking about a billionaire flying to space in July of 2021 as they did discussing the climate crisis in all of 2020. This illustrates a sad fact about our media machine: it's not the most truthful or pressing stories that get attention, but rather those that collectively entertain or outrage us.

The truth is, the flight was nothing more than a joyride for Jeff Bezos and his midlife crisis—making it three miles above the Kármán line and enjoying about three minutes of weightlessness. Whereas the truth about climate change is that the increasing concentration of carbon dioxide in our atmosphere is warming our planet's surface temperature and melting 279 billion tons of Antarctic ice per year.

So while climate change threatens our quality of life and the actual lives of millions who live at or below sea level, we're paying attention to a billionaire launching himself into space. At least he said, "Thanks to all the Amazon Prime subscribers." If this doesn't demonstrate our gross idolatry of tech innovators, I don't know what does.

32

Morning Show Airtime Allocated to Bezos in Space vs. the Climate Crisis

Sources: Media Matters for America; images: EDIE, DOGO News.

CHAPTER 4

Hunger Games

Inequality is inherent to the market, but when wealth is entrenched and mobility suppressed, that's cronyism, not capitalism.

Forty years of economic growth has created vast wealth. But the same structural and cultural changes that generated that wealth also determined its allocation. We made shareholder returns the sole metric of success, and so shareholders are the most successful. We lauded the individual at the head of the organization for his (almost always his) genius, and so that individual garners the greatest share of the organization's production. We acclaimed the power of technology, and so technology has gained the most power.

As I write this, 8 of the 10 wealthiest people in the world are current or former CEOs of American technology companies, and their wealth consists almost entirely of shareholdings in those companies. *Time*'s reigning Person of the Year, Elon Musk, is the richest of the eight. Between 1990 and 2021, the top 1% of households increased their share of the nation's wealth from 24% to 32%.

Outside the gilded mansions of the elite, this era of prosperity feels very different. For the past fifty years, income growth for middle- and low-income households has been sluggish. Income for the bottom quintile of households is up 14% since 1975—that's compared to a 109% increase for the top quintile. It's true that in some areas these limited dollars buy more than ever before—$10 a month for Netflix provides access to $17 billion in annual content, and there's never been so many different kinds of sneakers for sale. But that's cold comfort when healthcare, education, and housing take ever deeper bites of a stagnating income. Americans are burdened by $1.7 trillion of student loan debt.

What turns this from bad to terrible, what makes it un-American, is that these advantages are becoming entrenched. The elites are digging in, protecting their growing fortunes from the risks of the very markets they claim to support. Bailouts, tax breaks, and subsidies are the tools of entrenchment. Our capitalism has become cronyism: rugged individualism on the way up, but socialism on the way down.

The result? The American Dream used to be to work hard and do better than your parents. But today a thirty-year-old isn't doing as well as their parents were at thirty. The new American Dream is to be born rich.

Poor kindergartners with good scores are less likely to graduate from high school, graduate from college, or earn a high wage than their affluent peers with bad grades. Sixty-one percent of kids from families earning more than $100,000 a year attend a four-year university, compared to only 39% of students from families earning less than $30,000. At thirty-eight colleges, including five of the Ivies, there are more students from the top 1% of the U.S. income scale than from the bottom 60%.

In a healthy capitalist economy wealth is always at risk. Competition spurs innovation, disrupts the established order, and creates winners—but also losers. Joseph Schumpeter called it the "gale of creative destruction." But today in America, those who've benefited from prior storms have suppressed that gale, stifling creativity and competition.

The Great Divergence

Corporate profits used to track employee compensation. When companies had good years, pay increased for both management and regular employees. When there were bad years, both suffered. Around the time of the dot-com boom, however, corporate profits started to diverge from employee compensation. Specifically, they started rising faster. They dipped when the bubble burst in 2001, but ramped up again quickly thereafter. Now there are two distinct lines. Corporate profits keep skyrocketing, while employee compensation achieves mild increases. Since 1960, corporate profits have grown 85-fold; employee compensation, 38-fold.

What we're doing is effectively protecting and rewarding existing shareholders, while diminishing opportunities for future innovators. To "protect" existing shareholders, we're making them immune to disruption. Since 2000, U.S. airlines have declared bankruptcy sixty-six times, and the boards and CEOs of the six largest airlines have spent 96% of their free cash flow on share buybacks, which increase share price and thus management compensation. Then, when Covid disrupted air travel, the federal government gave $50 billion of taxpayers' money to the airline industry.

Bailouts of $50 billion to companies like Delta, whose CEO earned $13 million in 2020, or healthcare for low-income seniors, healthcare for veterans, and vocational programs for underserved high schoolers? America has made its choice.

33

Index of Corporate Profits After Tax and Compensation of Employees

Indexed to 1960

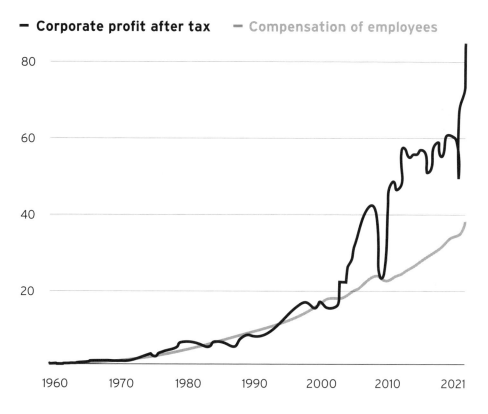

— **Corporate profit after tax**   — Compensation of employees

Source: Federal Reserve Bank of St. Louis.

It's Wealthy at the Top

It makes sense that a CEO is generally the highest paid employee of any company, but the growing discrepancy between CEO and average worker compensation does not. In 1965, the chiefs of America's largest 350 companies by revenue made 21 times the average compensation of their industries' workers. In 2020, the CEO-to-worker compensation ratio shot to 351:1, up 1,670% since 1965.

Calculating CEO pay is complicated by the role of stock-based compensation. Defenders of high pay claim that stock-heavy compensation renders high pay the result of high performance. But does it? Why should a sustained bull market lead to massive pay increases for the CEO (and not the workers)? Because in the church of shareholder value, a rising stock price is the one true god.

34

CEO-to-Worker Compensation Ratio

Top 350 American companies by revenue

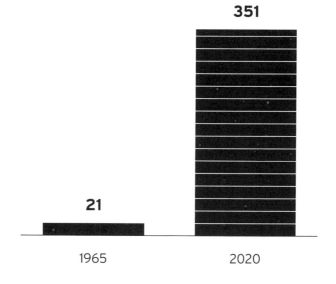

Source: Economic Policy Institute.

From Lopsided to Dystopian

In 1990, the wealthiest 1% of Americans controlled more than their fair
share. Fast-forward thirty-one years, and the distribution of wealth in
America has gone from lopsided to dystopian. By 2021, 50% of Americans
controlled only 2% of the nation's wealth, and the richest 1% had almost a
third. Wealth inequality has also worsened globally. The rich have gotten
richer by taking wealth from the bottom half of income earners. By the
end of 2019, the top 1% of the adult population accounted for 44% of global
net worth.

America's secret sauce used to be the balance between free market
policies and anticompetition regulations. However, as regulation has
become demonized and our titans have become likable tech CEOs,
we've relaxed our stance—to the detriment of our middle class.

When societies become intensely unequal, the discontented majority
usually rises up. If we continue on our chosen path, I worry this
will happen in America. In fact, it already has. The January 6, 2021,
insurrection was about feeling disconnected and robbed.

35

Distribution of Net Wealth in the U.S.

Bottom 50%   Top 1%

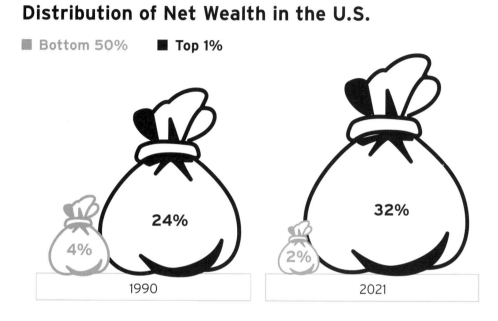

Source: Federal Reserve Bank of St. Louis.

Invasive Species

Value is now so concentrated in the tech sector that six companies—
Meta (Facebook), Amazon, Apple, Netflix, Alphabet (Google), and
Microsoft—account for more than 20% of the S&P 500.

Over the past decade, advertisers have rushed toward digital, where apex
predators (Google and Facebook) take 2 out of every 3 dollars. Consumers
have followed, and now Amazon takes 1 out of 3 e-commerce dollars.
Netflix spends $17 billion on content annually, enough to make 1,133
episodes of *Game of Thrones*. That's a lot of dragons.

These businesses were accumulating power long before Covid, but the
pandemic acted as an accelerant. When physical encounters suddenly
became dangerous, Big Tech stepped in with socially distant ways to
order essential items, work, socialize, and be entertained. And as it
evolves from being a pandemic to an endemic disease, Covid promises
to finish the takeover job the search and social firms started.

36

FAANMG* Market Capitalization Share of the S&P 500

■ **FAANMG**   ■ Rest of S&P 500

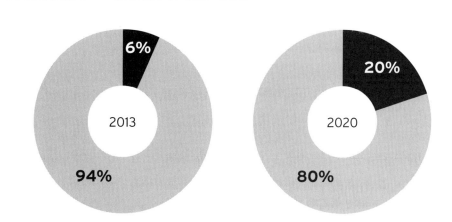

Source: Yardeni Research, Inc.

Note: *Facebook, Apple, Amazon, Netflix, Microsoft, and Google.

The Minimum Wage Is Decades Behind

In 1950, the federal minimum wage was $0.75 per hour, or $8.51 in 2021 dollars. But today, the legal minimum is only $7.25 per hour. This effective cut to minimum wage has come even though workers are much more productive than they were seventy years ago. In fact, had minimum wage climbed along with worker productivity, it would have been $22.18 per hour by 2021.

To put that into context, the inflation-adjusted median cost of a home in 1950 was $87,524, and the median cost of a home today is over $400,000. It's in this market that workers are supposed to live on $1.26 less per hour than they would have made in the 1950s.

This just doesn't make sense. As of 2021, in almost all urban and rural areas of the country, a single adult without children working full time must earn more than $15 per hour to sufficiently cover housing and other basic living expenses. Raising the minimum wage to $15 by 2025 would increase the earnings of 32 million workers, or 21% of the workforce, and lift up to 3.7 million people—including an estimated 1.3 million children—out of poverty.

Today, America is more feudal than democratic. One man—Jeff Bezos—has enough capital to end homelessness in the U.S. ($20 billion), eradicate malaria worldwide ($90 billion), and pay 700,000 teachers' salaries. Bezos makes the average Amazon employee's annual salary every ten seconds. Yes, we are a country that rewards genius, but we used to be one that showed kindness and generosity to those in need.

37

Federal Minimum Wage and Value If It Had Risen with Total Economic Productivity

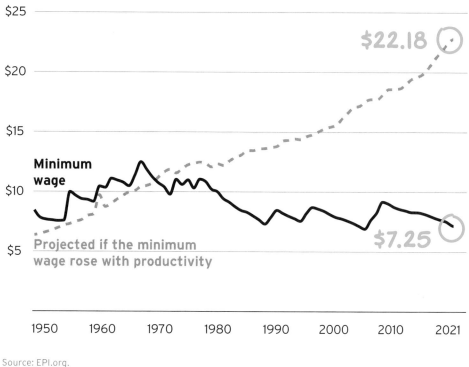

Source: EPI.org.

Note: Based on 2021 dollars.

What Are Our Priorities?

Between 1993 and 2020, the price of education skyrocketed, while the costs of food, housing, and medical care also rose substantially. What didn't go up? Real incomes. Of course, a $500 television you buy today is incomparably better than a television you could buy at any price in 1995, and the least expensive modern smartphone had no comparable product in 1995.

It's not a bad thing that clothes are cheaper and televisions are better. But those advances obscure that it's gotten a lot harder for average families to make ends meet, and a lot harder to get their children the education they need to climb up the income ladder.

38

Consumer Price Index for All Urban Consumers by Category vs. Real Median Income

Indexed to 1993

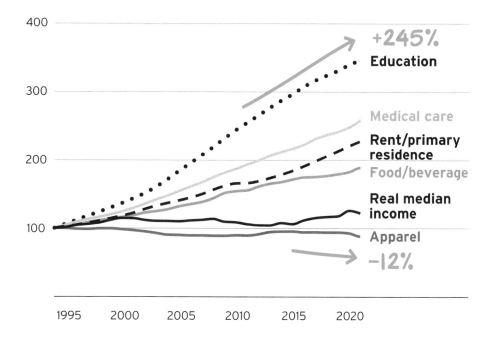

+245%

Education

Medical care

Rent/primary residence

Food/beverage

Real median income

Apparel

−12%

Source: Federal Reserve Bank of St. Louis.

Financialization and Asset Inflation

America has never had such a disconnect between Main Street and Wall Street, or the real economy and the financial economy. Prior to 1980, America's total financial assets never surpassed two times the nation's GDP. That ratio has trended higher ever since, spiking to a high of 5.9:1 at the onset of the pandemic. This increased financialization has been driven by a multitude of factors, including unprecedented money printing and Wall Street's ceaseless ability to create new financial products such as mortgage-backed securities and other weapons of mass financial destruction. This is also a global phenomenon: The total value of financial assets held by the ten countries with the largest GDPs leapt from $290 trillion in 2000 to an astounding $1,020 trillion in 2020. That's over a quadrillion dollars, a number I didn't know existed until five minutes ago. Over the same period, the value of real assets grew from $160 trillion to $520 trillion.

The benefits of financialization are not widespread, largely accruing to asset holders and those working in the financial sector. More importantly, financialization continues to elevate the significance of the markets at the expense of the real world. This might explain why our pandemic response decided to bail out companies, when we should've been bailing out people.

39

U.S. Financial Assets Relative to GDP

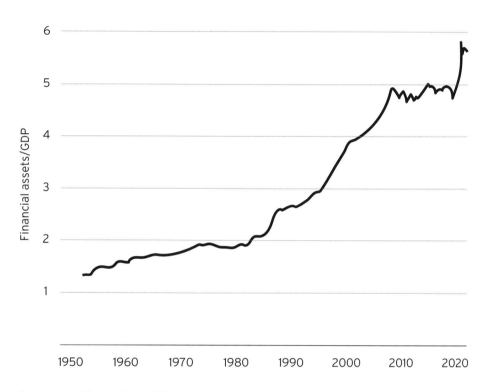

Source: Federal Reserve Bank of St. Louis.

Asset Inflation Comes Home

Policies that favor the redistribution of wealth from the young to the old have made it increasingly difficult for new generations to establish financial security. We can see this in the ratio of the median home value to the median household income over time. From 1960 through 1990, the median home price was equal to roughly two and a half years of household income. But by 2020 that ratio had nearly doubled: House prices were more than four times annual incomes.

Home ownership is a principal tenet of the American Dream. Owning a home builds credit, reduces housing costs, and makes a young family feel a sense of pride, belonging, and accomplishment. The home ownership rate in the U.S. peaked before the Great Recession, at almost 70%. Buying a home was cheap, compared to previous eras, and Americans took advantage. Since the disruption of the Great Recession, housing prices have skyrocketed. Older Americans reap the benefits of tax-deductible mortgage interest, while younger generations and the less wealthy are stuck paying nondeductible rent. We effectively transferred wealth from the young to the old.

40

Years of Median Household Income Equal to Median Home Sale Price

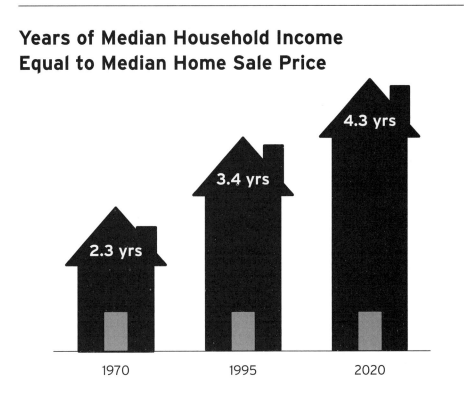

Source: Prof G analysis of Federal Reserve Bank of St. Louis data.

An Assault on America's Prosperity

The greatest assault on middle-class America's prosperity may be the relentless, four-decade-long inflation in higher education. Between 1980 and 2019, college costs increased 169%, while earnings for young workers rose just 19%.

This doesn't mean young people should skip college. In fact, a college degree is more necessary than ever before: Today, 2 out of 3 jobs require a postsecondary education and training, while in the 1970s, only 1 out of 4 required a degree. The bottom line: college degrees have grown more important and more expensive, while the ROI has gotten worse.

Americans' total student loan debt ($1.7 trillion) is now greater than their credit card debt. And that doesn't account for the busted 401(k)s, second mortgages, and general financial oppression my industry has levied on lower- and middle-income households.

41

Change in College Costs vs. Earnings for Young Workers

Constant 2019 dollars

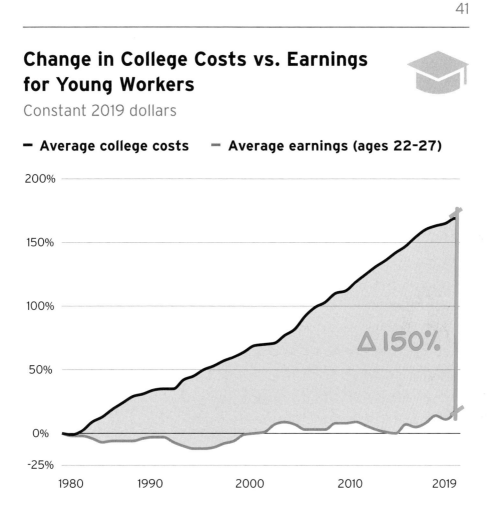

— **Average college costs**　— **Average earnings (ages 22-27)**

Source: Georgetown University Center on Education and the Workforce.

Another Covid Crime

When students finally returned to school in the fall of 2021, many had experienced over a year of remote learning. Teachers found that all children had fallen behind—students were five months off the learning pace they would have experienced but for Covid.

The effect was greater in schools with more Black or Hispanic students and more low-income families. Students at these schools started the pandemic as much as nine months behind students in majority-white, higher-income schools. By December of 2021, McKinsey assessed that majority-Black schools had fallen a full year behind majority-white schools.

The effects of pandemic school closures will be wide reaching, especially for younger children. Students who do not learn to read proficiently by third grade have difficulty catching up and are four times less likely to graduate from high school. This could affect the lifetime achievement of millions of students and even the economic, scientific, and creative achievements of our country.

42

Months Behind in School in Reading and Math Due to Pandemic

U.S. grades 1-6, fall 2020-21, number of months behind historical peers

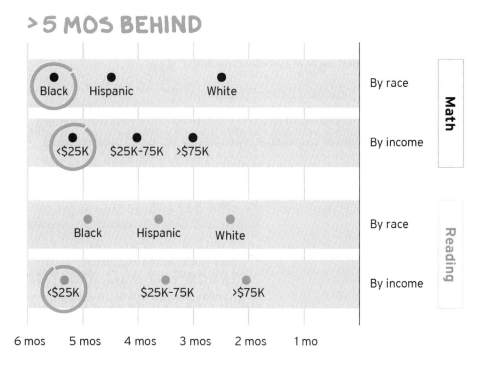

Source: Curriculum Associates I-Ready Assessment Data via McKinsey.

The U.S. Healthcare System Is Embarrassingly Inefficient

Healthcare costs per capita in the U.S. are among the highest in the world; yet our life expectancy is lower than those of most other developed nations. We lag behind Australia, Israel, the Netherlands, Portugal, Switzerland, and the U.K., and their healthcare is cheaper than ours.

Healthcare in this country is slow, inefficient, expensive, and ripe for disruption. The U.S. healthcare industry accounts for 45% of all medical spending globally. We spend almost 18% of our GDP on it, more than any other country. Yet our outcomes are worse. Sixty-four percent of patients say they've avoided or delayed medical care out of concern for the price tag. No wonder—the top one hundred hospitals, on average, charged patients seven times the cost of service.

What's generating this combination of inflated costs and bad outcomes? Administrative bloat is part of it. We spend more than $800 billion a year on healthcare administration in the U.S., more than the GDP of Saudi Arabia. Almost a third of that, $265 billion, is spent on regulatory and administrative tasks. That's more than the U.S. spends treating cancer. We cured polio, put astronauts on the moon, and developed three Covid vaccines in record time—we are better than our current healthcare system.

43

Life Expectancy vs. Healthcare Expenditure by Country

2015

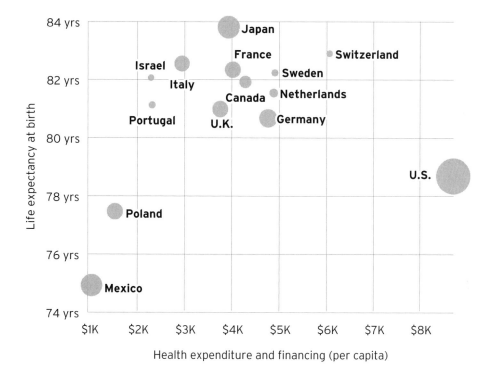

Source: World Bank via Our World in Data.

Note: Scale of circles indicates average annual change 1970 – 2015.

Waking Up From the American Dream

For the first time in U.S. history, young people are no longer better off economically than their parents were at the same age. An American born in 1940 had a 92% chance of doing better than his or her parents. Someone born in 1970 had a 61% chance. A millennial born in 1984, who'd be thirty-seven today, only has a 50% chance.

I worry about the effects of age-based inequality. Immigrants, like my parents, come to America so their kids can make better lives for themselves. That used to be attainable. Now young people are fed up. They have less than half of the economic security, as measured by the ratio of wealth to income, that their parents did at the same age. Their share of wealth has crashed. I believe that fading economic opportunity and mobility is a disease, and the symptoms are shame, frustration, and rage. Young people—men in particular—have already found outlets for those feelings: chat rooms on Reddit, meme stocks, and violent protests are all signs of burgeoning boredom and frustration.

44

Percentage of 30-Year-Olds Earning More Than Their Parents Did at 30

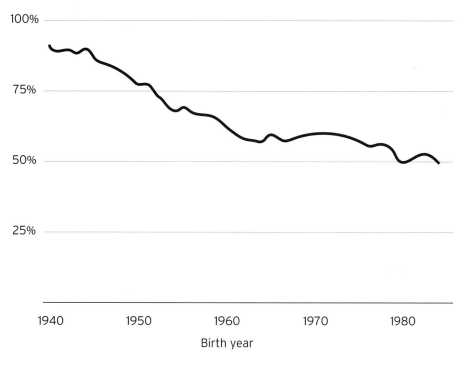

Birth year

Source: *Science*, December 2016.

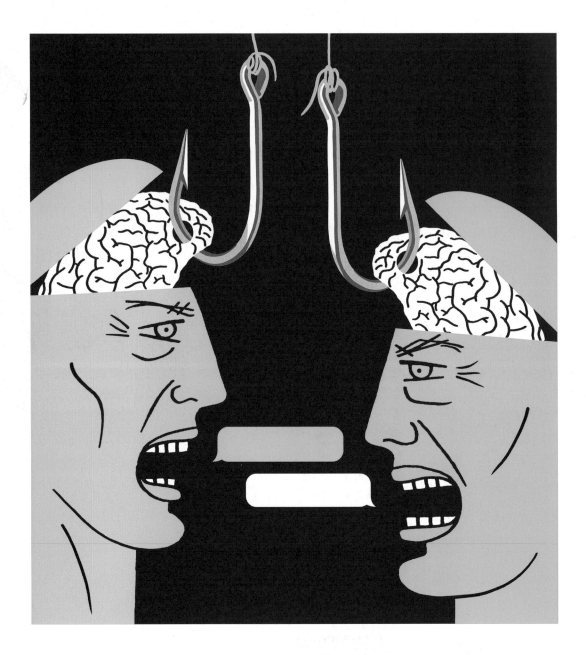

CHAPTER 5

The Attention Economy

If you are not paying, then you are not the customer. You are the product.

On January 9, 2007, Steve Jobs took the stage at MacWorld and announced that Apple was making a phone. He called it a "revolutionary product ... that changes everything." He was right, it would. We just didn't realize how.

At the time, pundits were questioning the decision of a three-year-old startup called Facebook to pass on a $900 million buyout offer from Yahoo!. A podcasting company called Odeo was at South by Southwest marketing its new product, Twitter.

Though the consumer internet boom began in the late 1990s, it was another decade before the real paradigm shift arrived. The twin forces of mobile and social changed everything. We started evaluating companies not by revenue but by users. We started comparing the population of Facebook to the populations of nations (a comparison it quickly outgrew). We saw more and more internet brands we didn't actually buy anything from—we just used them for free. They were free because we weren't the customer. We had become the product.

In 2010, we spent 3% of our waking hours on our phones. In 2021, that number was 33%. More than half of that time is spent on social media, and many of the world's largest companies are almost entirely subsidized by the monetization of our attention. Over 80% of Alphabet's revenue comes from advertising. At Meta, it's 98%. Together they bring in more than a third of total advertising revenue in the U.S. This shift transpired within a decade.

It was a shift enabled by algorithms—the systems that decide
what comes up next on the endless scroll of social media. And
what those algorithms have figured out is that the content that
garners the most attention is that which enrages us. YouTube
videos identified as disturbing by users receive 70% more
views than the average video. Falsehoods spread on Twitter
at six times the speed of truth. Facebook refers members to
untrustworthy news sources more than 15% of the time.

The internet was built on promises of uniting us in a more
socially connected world. It has had the opposite effect. We are
a house divided—siloed in our echo chambers, no longer in sync.
My NYU colleague Jonathan Haidt says that successful
democracies are generally bound together by strong institutions,
shared stories, and wide social networks with high levels of
trust, but social media weakens all three. Somewhere, in our
daze of posting, liking, and tweeting, we've lost the plot.

We're All Addicted to Our Phones

American Gen Zers unlock their phones almost eighty times per day. And they aren't alone. Our phones have become essential extensions of our identities, and that attachment formed remarkably quickly. The iPhone was released in 2007, and about half of American adults had a smartphone by 2012. Fast-forward less than a decade, and almost half of Americans feel some degree of anxiety when they don't have their phone. A 2020 study found that 96% of Gen Z Americans won't go to the bathroom without their phone. Daily phone use has been increasing by 25% per year since 2010. Today, the average American spends 4 hours and 23 minutes of every day using their mobile device.

We eat and drink three or four times a day. Most adults laugh seventeen times per day. A study of over 26,000 people from 1989 to 2014 found that the average adult has sex about once a week. That means, in an average week, a young adult might have sex once, laugh about 120 times, and unlock their phone more than 550 times.

Technology has never been so integrated into the human experience.

45

Average Unlocks per Day Among U.S. Smartphone Users

2018

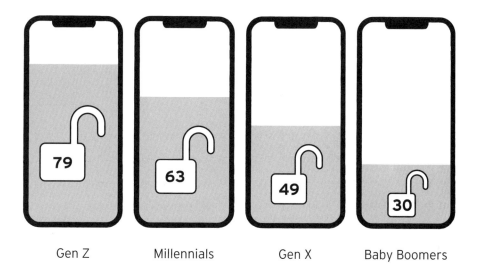

Gen Z · Millennials · Gen X · Baby Boomers

Source: Verto Analytics via Statista.

Digital Billboards

The explosion of screen time was fueled by a business model that at one point didn't seem viable and was largely misunderstood: advertising. The notion of subsidizing an algorithmic search engine that crawls through 37 trillion gigabytes of data and delivers personalized results ranked by relevance within 0.2 seconds on tiny virtual billboards was a dubious business plan when Google first launched. What we neglected to consider, however, was the power of scale.

More users combined with more time spent on devices turned the digital advertising industry into a cash behemoth. In 2011, digital ads accounted for a fifth of all advertising revenue in the U.S. Since then, nondigital shrunk and digital exploded. Digital ads now drive 63% of all ad revenue in America, and they've turned advertising into a nearly $250 billion industry.

46

U.S. Advertising Revenue

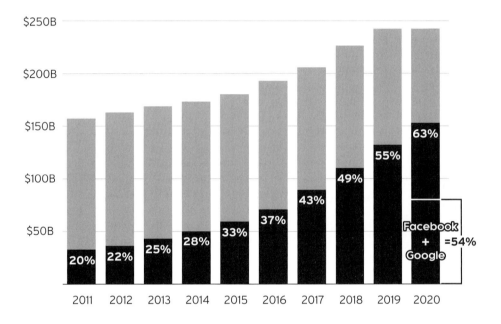

Sources: eMarketer, Pew Research Center.

Decline of the News

As our time got swallowed up by Facebook and Google, we stopped paying attention to the media that once mattered most to us—particularly the news. In 2008, U.S. newspapers generated $38 billion in ad revenue. That number fell 27% the next year and continued to plummet. In 2020, newspaper ad revenue came out to less than $9 billion, a record low.

With falling revenue came a dwindling pool of journalists. In 2008, the number of newsroom employees across all channels in the U.S.— from print to television—was roughly 114,000. By 2020 that number had fallen 26%, to 85,000. If the number of American journalists served as a proxy measurement for our nation's collective truth, the truth was in sharp decline.

47

Newspaper Ad Revenue and Newsroom Employees

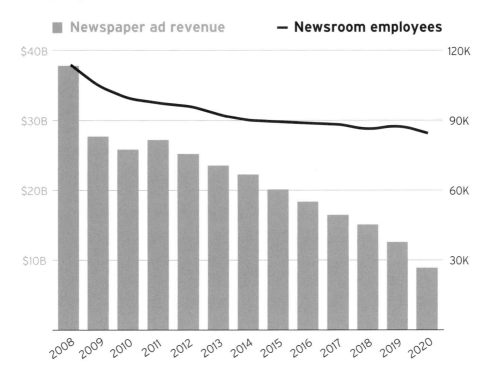

Sources: Pew Research Center, News Media Alliance, Bureau of Labor Statistics.

Triggered

New social media apps like Instagram and Twitter soon entered the fold, and our attention spans continued to diminish. By 2014, 55% of website visits lasted less than fifteen seconds. For news outlets, the majority of which are still heavily subsidized by ads, that meant adjusting the headlines to maintain our attention. The best news stories are the ones that garner the most clicks, likes, and shares. In the previous era of news, the only trackable performance metric was print sales, but the internet allows journalistic institutions to measure what drives readership down to the individual headline. It soon became clear that virality was directly correlated with emotion: the most popular headlines are ones that disturb, shock, and enrage us.

Researchers from the Wharton business school performed a statistical analysis of the social transmission of *New York Times* articles— specifically, which content characteristics provided the greatest likelihood of an article making the paper's most-emailed list. Three characteristics ensured virality more than any others. For every standard deviation increase of anxiety elicited, the probability of an article making the most-emailed list went up by 21%. For awe, it went up 30%. But the most powerful emotion was anger, increasing virality by 34%.

48

Probability of Making the *New York Times* Most-Emailed List by Emotion Elicited

2012

+21%

+30%

+34%

Anxiety

Awe

Anger

Source: Jonah Berger, Katherine Milkman. "What Makes Online Content Viral?" *Journal of Marketing Research,* April 2012.

Liar, Liar

While journalistic institutions began sensationalizing headlines in an effort to keep their budgets and newsrooms from emptying any further, a novel form of "news" was emerging—only this one wasn't subject to any editorial scrutiny and possessed the viral potential of the common cold: Twitter.

Between 2010 and 2015, Twitter's monthly active user base grew tenfold, from 30 million to 300 million. As was the case for institutional news outlets, the most popular tweets were the ones that triggered our most violent emotions. For journalists, that meant dramatizing the news. For Twitter users, it meant making it up.

An MIT study examined a data set of 126,000 tweets in all categories of information—from science to terrorism to finance—and sorted them based on factual accuracy. The time taken for falsehoods to reach 1,500 people, they found, was six times shorter than it was for the truth. Meanwhile, 7 in 10 U.S. adult Twitter users say they get news on the site, and 80% of all tweets come from 10% of its users.

49

The Speed of Lies

Based on average time to reach 1,500 users on Twitter

Falsehood spreads

6X faster

than the truth on Twitter

Source: *Science*, March 2018.

"Political" Censorship

The proliferation of lies on social media platforms has led to widespread distrust of the social media companies themselves: More than 7 in 10 Americans believe social media sites censor political views.

That distrust has widened across party lines. Nine in every 10 Republicans suspect political censorship, vs. 6 in 10 Democrats. The reality of censorship on social media, however, has little to do with politics and everything to do with algorithms.

Because of the way posts are algorithmically ranked and recommended (i.e., optimized for engagement), the only content social media really censors is the stuff that bores us. In terms of reach, the less moderate and more partisan the content, the better. Sixty-four percent of people who join extremist groups on Facebook do so because the algorithm steers them there. Less than three years after QAnon appeared online, half of Americans had heard of its conspiracy theories. In reality, what social media favors is that which divides us.

50

Portion of Americans Who Think Social Media Sites Likely Censor Political Views

2020

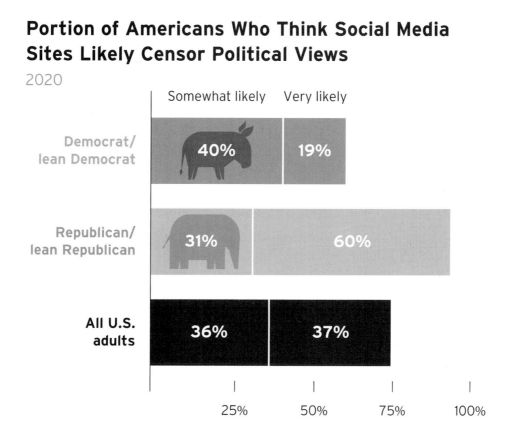

Somewhat likely   Very likely

**Democrat/
lean Democrat**   40%   19%

**Republican/
lean Republican**   31%   60%

**All U.S.
adults**   36%   37%

25%   50%   75%   100%

Fake News

In a digital world awash in extremism, misinformation, and conspiracy theories, distrust has spread into media at large, especially the cable networks. Between 2016 and 2021, Americans' trust in national news organizations suffered a sharp decline. This trend, like so many others in this decade, was acutely divided across party lines.

In five years, the share of Democrats who trust national news organizations fell 5%. Among Republicans, the drop was 35%. Today, less than 6 in 10 Americans trust the information that comes from national news organizations, and our confidence in newspapers and television news is at an all-time low.

51

Portion of Americans Who Trust Information From National News Organizations

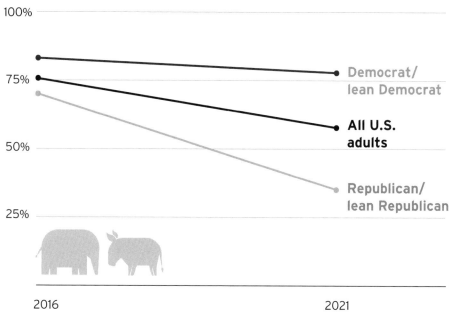

Source: Pew Research Center.

Media Fuels Misunderstanding About Crime

During the later years of the postwar era, violent crime began to rise in the U.S., a trend that continued until the early 1990s. By then it had become a central political issue. But in the wake of sustained economic prosperity, violent crime fell as quickly as it had risen—and it continues to fall, though its decline has slowed in recent years.

The reasons are murky, and credit is most likely due to a variety of factors, from an aging population to environmental protections (the reduction of lead pollution may have played a major role) to investments in police to better job prospects to diversion programs. As interesting as why crime fell, however, is the peculiar persistence of our perception that it *hasn't*. In 20 of 24 Gallup surveys conducted since 1993, at least 60% of U.S. adults each year think there is more crime nationally than the year before.

What explains this? Politicians love "tough on crime" rhetoric, and crime coverage drives news readership. "If it bleeds, it leads," goes the old adage. The Brennan Center found that *The New York Times* included "homicide" or "murder" in 129 headlines in 1990, when the homicide rate in New York City was 31 per 100,000 people. In 2013, when the murder rate had fallen to just 4 per 100,000, the *Times* had more headline references to homicide and murder: 135. In a social-media-driven future, there's little reason to hope that we'll trend away from sensationalism in crime coverage.

52

Perception vs. Reality of U.S. Crime Rate

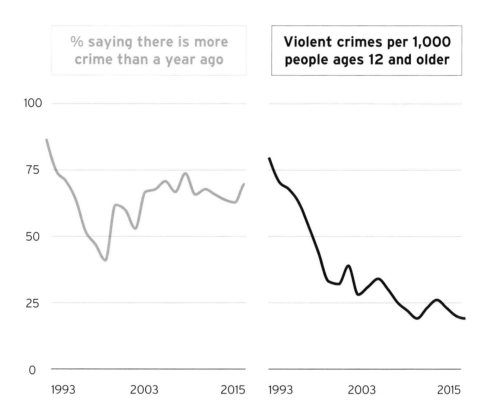

% saying there is more crime than a year ago

Violent crimes per 1,000 people ages 12 and older

Source: Pew Research Center.

Relationship Status

Spending more time on screens means investing more of our lives in online platforms—including our love lives. Throughout modern history, the most common way partners got together in America was through friends. When online "dating" (really, online *meeting*) began to gather momentum in the dot-com era, it tore through the cultural ecosystem, and within a generation it had become the dominant matchmaking medium.

There's a lot to be said for online connections. As with other forms of social media, it creates meaningful connections between people who would never have met in the physical world alone. It can make small towns feel bigger, by expanding personal networks, and big cities feel smaller, by connecting people with common interests.

But the perils of online dating have inspired as many tweets, think pieces, and research studies as the medium has formed couples. Suffice it to say, these platforms share the same flaws as any other that scales our instincts. Algorithms are indifferent to social interests or even true happiness.

53

Ways Romantic Partners Meet

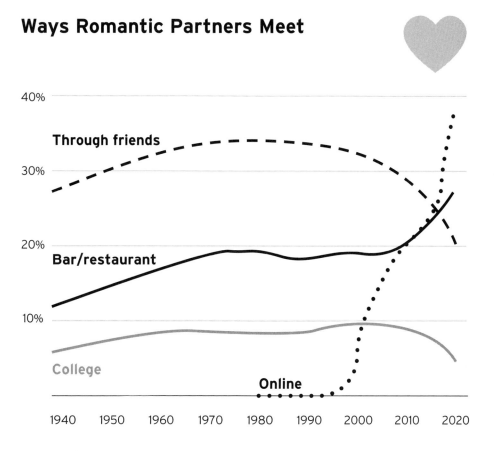

Source: Stanford University.

Note: Data based on heterosexual couples.

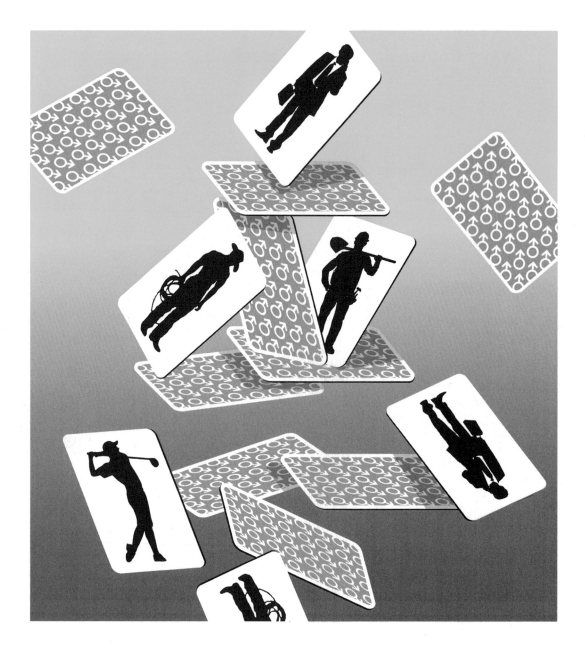

CHAPTER 6

House of Cards

Internal divisions have characterized the U.S. since its founding. Progress has come not from exploiting these fissures for private gain, but by knitting them together through shared prosperity.

In 2018, residents of a twelve-story condominium tower along
a beautiful stretch of the Florida coast reported evidence of
deterioration in the tower's concrete support slabs. Engineers
attempted to repair surface damage in 2020, but the project
was abandoned because of concerns that it would destabilize
the entire structure. In April 2021, there were more reports of
concrete deterioration, which was noted to be "much worse."
Remedial work was discussed and planned, but never begun.
Two months later, the Surfside, Florida, condo collapsed, killing
ninety-eight people.

In the aftermath of the Surfside tragedy, earlier images and
reports of pooling water, cracked concrete, and rusting rebar
were made public. The problems had been plain for all to see.
It's a familiar pattern. Warning signs are always obvious in the
rearview mirror. What are our warning signs? What are the
weaknesses in our foundation?

I'll start with one close to home. Men.

Based on a number of critical measures—education, economics,
and socialization—I see a crisis emerging for our young men.
While a privileged few (predominately older, white, and wealthy)
men wield a disproportionate amount of control in business,
politics, and society, many men are failing.

It begins early. Parents have higher educational expectations
for girls than for boys. Boys are twice as likely to be suspended
from school for the same offenses as girls, which correlates to
poorer educational outcomes. Across the U.S., the enrollment

of men in higher education institutions is two-thirds that of women, leading to limited professional opportunities and lower earning potential: men without a college education earn $900,000 less over their lifetime than college graduates.

Young men's ability to find and commit to a meaningful relationship is declining. Young people in America are living with their parents at rates not seen since the 1940s. The group that's seen the sharpest decline in marriage rates is poor men.

Research shows that declining marriage rates lead to lower economic output, reduced happiness, and a lower birth rate. A large and growing cohort of bored, lonely, poorly educated men is a malevolent force in any society, but it's a truly terrifying one in a society addicted to social media and awash in coarseness and guns.

We are also divided against ourselves, seeing enemies rather than adversaries in our politics. The moniker "United States of America" is a paradox today. A poll by the University of Virginia found that 2 out of 5 Biden voters believe it's time to split the country by party lines. Trump voters agree, with more than half favoring a breakup. Secession is the new *Succession*, and Texit the new Brexit.

This feeds a vicious cycle: As enemies, we cannot negotiate in good faith, and our government accomplishes nothing. Which further undermines our faith in government and fuels our hatred for our opponents.

Marriage Rates
Are at Record Lows

Marriage rates in the U.S., on the decline for decades, hit an all-time low
in 2020 of 5.1 per 1,000 people. That's lower than the 7.9 reported in 1932,
during the Great Depression.

The marriage rate has fallen faster at lower income levels. From 1970 to
2011, men in the bottom third of incomes were over 30% less likely to get
married, while marriage rates for men in the 85th percentile and higher
dropped less than 15%. Women at lower income rates have experienced
significant but slightly lower declines than men, while higher-income-
earning women have hardly seen their marriage rate decline at all—for
women earning the top 1% of income, it actually increased over the
period. Theirs was the only income cohort to see a rise in matrimony.

Marriage is a powerful institution. It gives us a partner—economically,
emotionally, and logistically. Two people form a more efficient household
and build a stronger foundation that consistently proves to produce better
outcomes for children. A household of unmarried parents makes just two-
thirds of the income a married couple makes. Married people have better
health insurance (as do their kids) and greater access to social networks
(via their spouse). So, not surprisingly, they tend to live longer, experience
fewer strokes and heart attacks, and have a lower incidence of depression.

54

Marriage Rates

Per 1,000 population

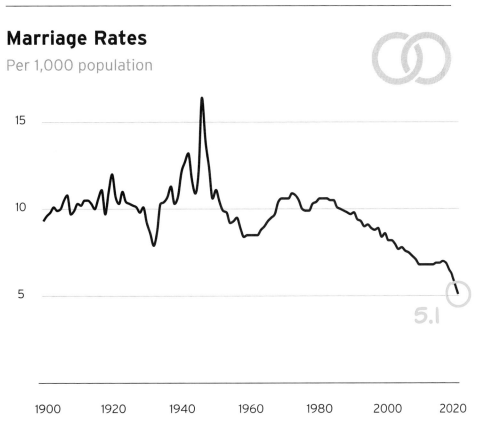

5.1

1900   1920   1940   1960   1980   2000   2020

Source: CDC.

Women Value Earning Potential in Male Partners

In a 2017 survey, over two-thirds of Americans, both men and women, said it's "very important" for a man to support his family financially to be considered a good partner. By contrast, only 25% of men say financial security is very important for a *woman* to be a good wife or partner (39% of women feel that way). The bottom line: We put dramatically different emphasis on men's and women's earning power.

55

Importance of Financial Security in Partners

O **Men who agree with statement**

O Women who agree with statement

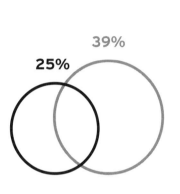

72%   71%

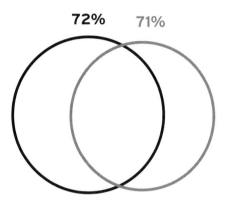

39%

25%

Being able to support a family
financially is very important for a
man to be a good husband/partner.

Being able to support a family
financially is very important for a
woman to be a good wife/partner.

Source: Pew Research Center.

Men's Share of College Enrollment at Record Lows

In 2021, men accounted for 40% of college enrollments, down from nearly 60% in 1970. In the 2018–19 academic year, more than 1.1 million women received a bachelor's degree, compared to fewer than 860,000 men. Fewer men going to college means fewer men on pathways to economic prosperity. More men getting off the ladder to prosperity means more men getting on the path to becoming what I consider the most dangerous cohort in America: broke and lonely males.

56

Men's Share of College Enrollment in the U.S.

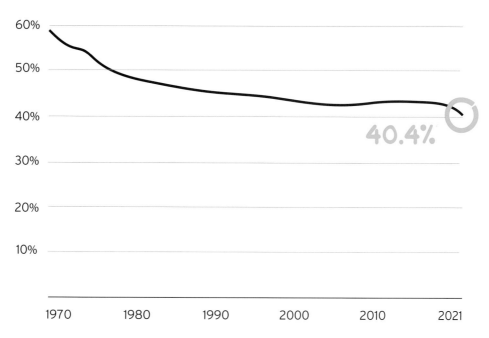

40.4%

Source: National Student Clearinghouse.

Online Dating Apps Are More Inequitable Than Almost Anywhere on Earth

Dating apps sort potential partners into a tiny group of haves and a titanic group of have-nots. The most attractive people on the platform score the largest share of matches, whereas the vast majority receive very few. To measure economic inequality in societies, economists use a Gini coefficient. Higher coefficients mean greater levels of inequality, and lower coefficients mean lower levels of inequality. As it pertains to likes received, heterosexual females and males on Hinge showed a Gini index of 0.38 and 0.54, respectively. Accordingly, if Hinge were an economy, it would rank among the most unequal places in the world.

57

Economic Inequality of Countries vs. Attractiveness Inequality on Hinge

2017

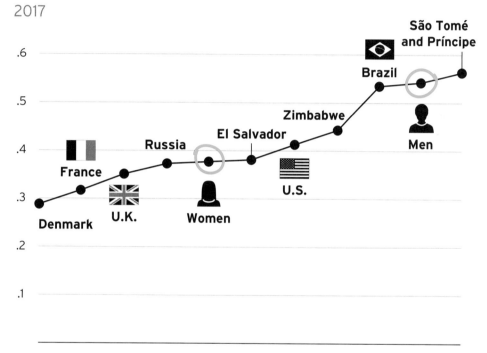

Source: Quartz.

Political Divides Become Social Divides

Parents' political beliefs might not be supporting marriage rates. (Especially if their children live under the same roof.) In 1960, 1 in 25 parents had concerns about their child marrying someone from the opposite political party. By 2018, almost half of Democratic parents and a third of Republican parents had such concerns.

58

Concerns About Child Marrying the Opposite Party

● **1960**   ● 2018

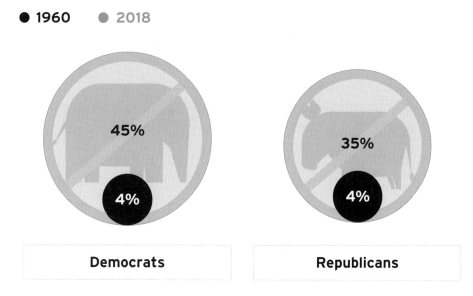

| Democrats | Republicans |

Source: Inter-University Consortium for Political and Social Research & Public Religion Research Institute.

Failure to Leave

With lower college enrollments, fewer pathways to economic security, and fewer intimate relationships being formed, young adults have less impetus and means to leave home. The share of young adults living with their parents reached its highest level on record in 2020. Prior to that peak, the highest measured value was in the 1940 census, at the end of the Great Depression, when 48% of young adults lived with their parents. By February 2020, the number was 47%, before Covid added accelerant to the trend and took it to 52%.

59

U.S. Share of 18- to 29-Year-Olds Living With Parents

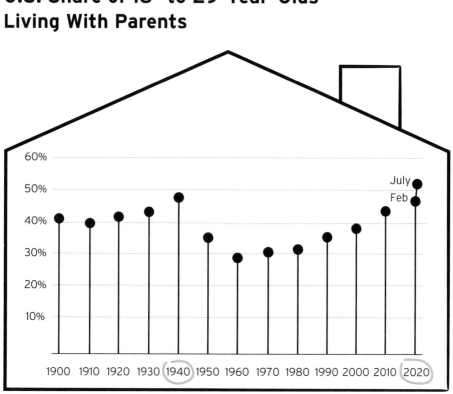

Source: Pew Research Center.

Population Growth Is Slowing to Great Depression Levels

Population growth is generally considered a prerequisite for economic growth: More people means more work, which means more economic value. As workers age and exit the workforce, they must be replaced by younger people or immigrants, to both provide for retirees and sustain the economy. But U.S. population growth is slowing. Between 2010 and 2020, the population grew just 7.4%, making it the decade with the slowest rate of expansion in U.S. history.

Unlike the temporary reduction in growth during the Depression, this slowdown is a result of fundamental transformations: Americans are having fewer children, and we have gradually narrowed the gateways of immigration. Population growth is a function of life span as well, and where we once experienced steadily lengthening lives, the so-called diseases of despair—drug overdoses, obesity, and suicide, which all accelerated during the Covid-19 pandemic—are taking a greater and greater toll every year.

60

U.S. Population Growth by Decade

Source: The Brookings Institution.

Created Equal

It's fundamental to the American promise that we are all created
equal. That promise, however, is broken from birth. Race, geography,
economic status, and more have profound impacts on a child's chances
for prosperity, even life. Being born a boy or a girl is perhaps the most
consequential of all.

Girls face threats from men and from a media that exploits their fears and
insecurities, and then, as women, they enter a working world where the
deck is stacked against them. Boys face threats, too, and these have been
getting more ominous in recent years. Deaths of despair stalk boys and
young men, and they are ill-prepared for these challenges by a culture
that mistakes braggadocio for masculinity, and aggression for strength.

61

Outlook at Birth by Gender

Girl

3x more likely to experience abuse

3x more likely to self-harm

Will earn **84¢ to 93¢** for every dollar a man earns

2x more likely to be passed up for a promotion as a parent

Boy

Less likely to graduate college

2x more likely to overdose

3.5x more likely to commit suicide

9x more likely to go to jail

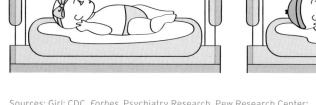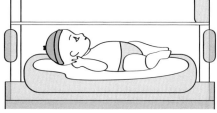

Sources: Girl: CDC, *Forbes*, Psychiatry Research, Pew Research Center; Boy: The Brookings Institution, Pew Research Center, AFSP, Federal Bureau of Prisons.

Mass Murder Is a Uniquely Male Crime

Bored young men without any pathway to economic security or a meaningful relationship aren't just dangerous to themselves, they're dangerous to society. A report by the U.S. Secret Service revealed that only 1 in 3 mass violent attackers in 2019 had symptoms of a mental illness, whereas 92% of them were male, and more than two-thirds were under the age of thirty-five.

As a species, we need physical and social contact, and we crave deep, meaningful bonds. Men who fail to attach to a partner, career, or community grow bitter and seek volatility and unrest. The loss of economic pathways for young people is no less serious for women, but it appears to be less dangerous. When young women feel shame and rage, they don't turn to semiautomatic weapons.

62

Demographics of Mass Shooters in the U.S.

2017-2019

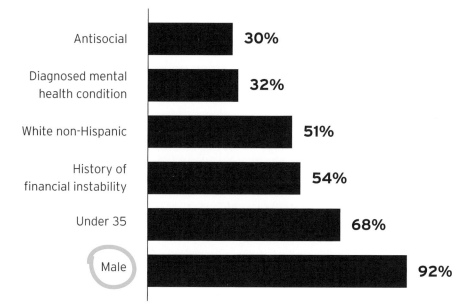

Antisocial	30%
Diagnosed mental health condition	32%
White non-Hispanic	51%
History of financial instability	54%
Under 35	68%
Male	92%

Source: U.S. Secret Service.

The Long-Term Erosion of Trust in the Federal Government

In a democracy that's been pushed to its limits by competing narratives and unfounded online theories about politicians and political agendas, it's no wonder that Americans seem to have lost faith in the people running the nation. The National Election Study began surveying the public about its trust in the government back in 1958—a time when about 75% of Americans trusted the federal government to do the right thing almost always or most of the time. That percentage hasn't surpassed 30% since 2007.

In 2021, 42% of Americans believed our political system needed to be completely overhauled, and another 43% said it required major changes. In contrast, only 12% to 15% of people in most Western European countries said their political systems should get a complete revamp.

63

Aggregate Public Opinion Polls
on Trust in U.S. Government

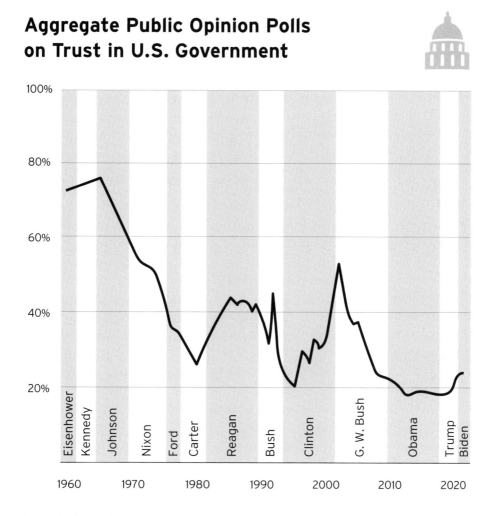

Source: Pew Research Center.

Old Money, Old Problems

One of the most stubborn inequalities in the U.S. remains the wealth gap between white and nonwhite households. For every dollar of wealth a typical white household has, a Black household has 12 cents, a divide that's *grown* over the past half-century. Hispanic households have 21 cents for every dollar in white wealth.

64

Median Household Wealth by Race

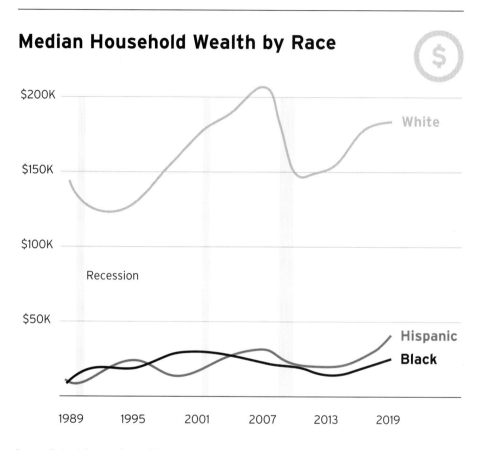

Source: Federal Reserve Bank of St. Louis, *New York Times*.

Those Funding the Future Reflect the Past

Startups and technology have been a disruptive force to traditional means of wealth creation. But the venture capitalists deciding which founders receive investment and reap the rewards of successful startups overwhelmingly are white men with similar backgrounds. In a 2018 survey, 8 in 10 venture capitalists were male, 7 in 10 were white, and 4 in 10 had a degree from Stanford or Harvard.

65

Venture Capital Diversity

2018

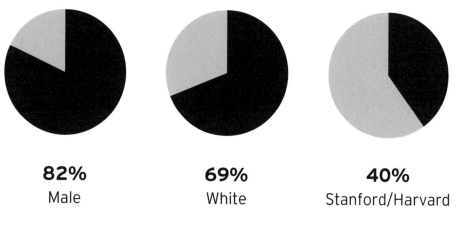

82%
Male

69%
White

40%
Stanford/Harvard

Sources: Richard Kerby, Equal Ventures.

CHAPTER 7

Threats

While America looks inward, a changing world may look elsewhere for leadership.

The U.S. has enjoyed the benefits of economic and military hegemony for decades, but that supremacy is in decline. Since the collapse of the Soviet Union, the U.S. has been the sole superpower. But as influential as we've been, American interests are no longer the organizing principle of international relations. The past three decades have been a period of fractious regional conflicts, largely hapless efforts by the U.S. to exercise state power at home and abroad, and corporate and private interests running unchecked.

The pandemic revealed the chinks in America's armor with painful clarity. Despite our vast resources, we were unable to wrestle with a virus one-tenth the size of the smallest dust particle. Meanwhile, our global peers saw far lower death rates and much less dissemination of polarizing misinformation. As I write this in January 2022, the pandemic is muscling up with new variants, and our infighting is only getting worse. Covid is just one of any number of possible health crises we face, which are themselves just variants of the many threats confronting the commonwealth.

If there were an Olympics for building hospitals during the pandemic, China would have collected the gold, silver, and bronze, while we were fighting over representation at the opening ceremonies. Our response under an apprentice masquerading as a president left a stain on our reputation as the undisputed superpower that persists despite President Biden's best dry-cleaning efforts. After thirty years of hegemony, we are once again in a bipolar world, and a superpower duopoly will again be the organizing principle. This time the countervailing force against the U.S. is China.

In the global business landscape, the rising red sea hasn't drowned America ... yet. Chinese manufacturing is dominant, and the growth of its trade network is outpacing that of the U.S., but we still command the strategic high ground in finance, innovation, and military/diplomatic power. Yet the trends are unmistakable—where Chinese labor was once preferred because of its low cost, it's now Chinese skill and expertise that are winning bids. Chinese companies still live below America's penthouse suite, but they're climbing the floors as surely as they're climbing the value chain.

The gravest threat may be one of our own making, because it looks more and more like the tide of prosperity that lifted all our boats was in fact the rising level of a warming sea. What every scientist not buying a Tesla with their fossil fuel paycheck will tell you is that the only questions remaining about the costs of climate change are how bad and how fast. Crises are inherently opportunities, however, and the larger the crisis, the bigger the market. Forget the metaverse, decarbonization will be the biggest economic opportunity for the rising generation. The "total addressable market" (the key to startup economics) is ... humanity. Let me pose a question: Will a nation of innovators and builders see this as the opportunity of the century, or will we slowly sink beneath the waves?

The United States Retains the Title

America's myriad challenges and weaknesses shouldn't be allowed to obscure its continued dominance as the globe's preeminent power. American enterprises account for the majority of the world's largest 100 companies, which in turn supports the unrivaled scale of the U.S. stock markets. Our national research and development spending amounts to 30% of the world's total, with American startups accounting for 50% of the world's unicorns. The U.S. has more billionaires than any nation. We've also won more Olympic medals than any other country, and have a bigger defense budget than the next ten countries combined. American goods and services account for almost a quarter of the world's GDP. These numbers are impressive, but the wheel of American supremacy is held together by a few linchpins. Without them, the wheels would come off ... quickly.

66

American Share of Global Metrics

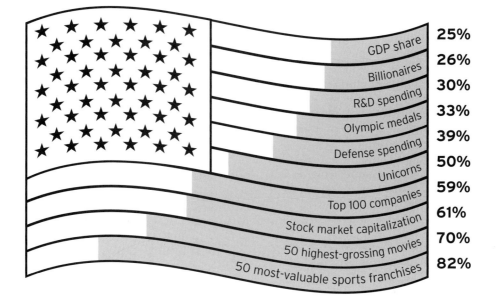

GDP share	25%
Billionaires	26%
R&D spending	30%
Olympic medals	33%
Defense spending	39%
Unicorns	50%
Top 100 companies	59%
Stock market capitalization	61%
50 highest-grossing movies	70%
50 most-valuable sports franchises	82%

Sources: World Bank, *Forbes*, The American Association for the Advancement of Science, NBC Sports, CB Insights, Lyn Alden Investment Strategy, IMDB.

The Dominance of the U.S. Dollar

The U.S. dollar accounts for almost 60% of global currency reserves, money that central banks around the world keep on hand to grease the wheels of international trade. America earned the privilege of becoming the world's reserve currency over half a century ago. Following World War II, the U.S. accounted for the majority of industrial production in the non-Soviet world, making it logical for the dollar to be the primary unit of exchange for international trade, invoicing, and loans. Under the Bretton Woods Agreement in 1944, America also promised to convert dollars brought by other countries' central banks into gold at a fixed rate, making the U.S. dollar the gold standard of currencies.

However, in 1971, Richard Nixon ended the convertibility of U.S. dollars into gold and made the dollar a fiat currency (a currency not backed by a commodity). America's Federal Reserve could now engage in monetary policy and money printing for the benefit of those within our borders, while exporting the consequences of our devalued currency to those outside. As Treasury Secretary John Connally famously told a group of finance ministers at the time, "The dollar is our currency, but your problem."

The dollar's dominance continues today, even though the U.S. "only" accounted for 25% of global GDP in 2020. The delta between that and global USD reserves (59%) can be thought of as America's "hegemon premium" (34%). But that premium is being challenged.

67

USD Share of Global Currency Reserves vs. U.S. Share of Global GDP

2020

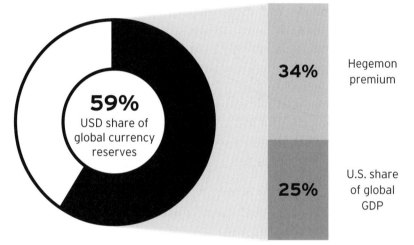

59%
USD share of
global currency
reserves

34% Hegemon
premium

25% U.S. share
of global
GDP

Sources: IMF, World Bank.

Note: USD share of global currency reserves as of Q2 2021.

China Has Replaced the U.S. as the Most Popular Trading Partner

An important contributor to political influence is economic interdependence. The U.S. was once the largest trading partner of the great majority of nations, but since 2000, China has superseded America in this regard. Today, three times as many nations call China their largest trade partner than can say that about the U.S. This trend will only be amplified by China's Belt and Road Initiative, an ambitious plan to expand Chinese economic connections throughout Asia, Africa, and Europe. The initiative covers 71 countries that account for more than half of the world's population and a third of global GDP. If that sounds like China elbowing out U.S. economic influence, trust your instincts.

68

Share of Countries With Largest Trade Partner: China vs. U.S.

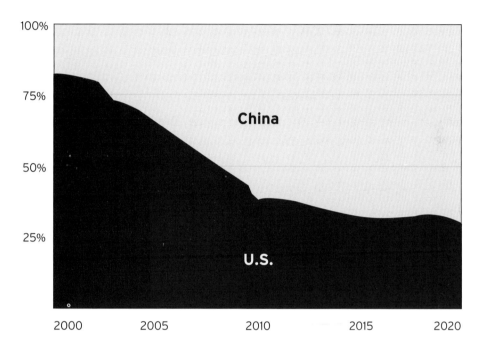

Sources: *Economist*, IMF.

The U.S. Gets Less for Its Military Dollar

In absolute terms, the U.S. defense budget accounts for over a third of the world's total defense spending, more than the combined expenditures of China, India, and Russia. But not all dollars are spent equally. When economists compare countries' GDP or standard of living, their common practice is to recognize local price differences. These fluctuations also apply to military spending. For example, labor costs for soldiers are far cheaper in China and India. Failing to account for these differences can lead to false confidence in American power.

Professor of economics and dean of the University of Western Australia Business School Peter Robertson addressed the differences in defense budgets by constructing a military purchasing power parity (MPPP) exchange rate based on each country's relative unit cost ratio.

The MPPP figures make America look far less dominant. On a nominal basis, China's spending is roughly $252 billion, only a third of America's. However, at MPPP it jumps to two-thirds of the U.S. budget. And this doesn't account for the asymmetric nature of modern warfare, where cyber capabilities and special operations of all kinds can have an outsized impact. In sum, military dollars can buy more in places where soldiers and equipment are cheaper.

69

Military Spending

■ **U.S.**   ⠿ **China**   ■ **India**   ▨ **Russia**

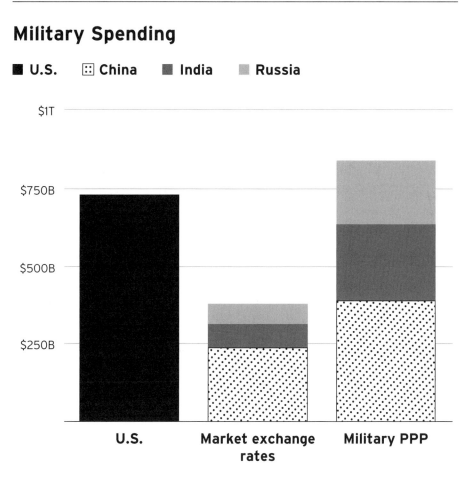

Source: Professor Peter Robertson, University of Western Australia.

Military Spending Doesn't Always Equate to Effectiveness

After the fall of the USSR, America's unrivaled defense spending, combined with its economic influence, meant it could project power so effectively that it largely won without fighting. The silent artillery of time has changed that, however, and America now seems to be fighting everywhere without winning, despite its enormous budget. The exit from Afghanistan demonstrated with startling clarity that a well-placed pawn can topple a king. If the U.S. defense budget were as tall as the Empire State Building, the entirety of Afghanistan's GDP would be only as high as the lampposts out front. The Taliban's income would be about the size of a fire hydrant.

70

U.S. Defense Spending vs. Afghanistan's GDP vs. Taliban's Income

2020

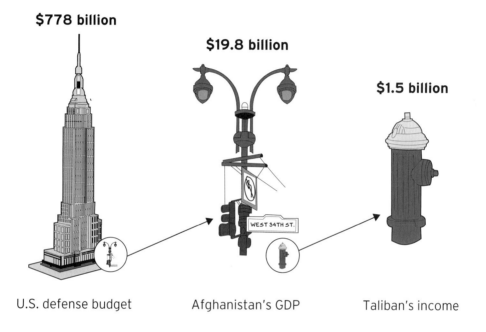

$778 billion

$19.8 billion

$1.5 billion

WEST 34TH ST.

U.S. defense budget   Afghanistan's GDP   Taliban's income

Sources: Stockholm International Peace Research Institute, World Bank, BBC.

Chinese Leadership in Military Drones

Beyond their military spending, rival nations garner power by exporting the fruits of that spending: defense technologies. On the frontier of defense tech, unmanned aerial weapons are reshaping the battlefield, and China is providing the ammunition. Over the past decade, it's delivered 220 drones to 16 countries.

There are several implications to this, not least of them the arms race it may spur and the potential for widespread human-rights abuses. By becoming the world's drone store, China can realize greater economies of scale. The prices for its drones are estimated at between $1 million and $2 million, while American units sell for as much as $15 million. Moreover, those drones will be tested more often in a wider variety of situations, and their Chinese manufacturers will be able to incorporate lessons from that experience into future manufacturing, improving effectiveness and bringing down costs.

71

Number of U.S.-Supplied vs. Chinese-Supplied Combat Drones

■ **U.S.-supplied drones**   ■ Chinese-supplied drones

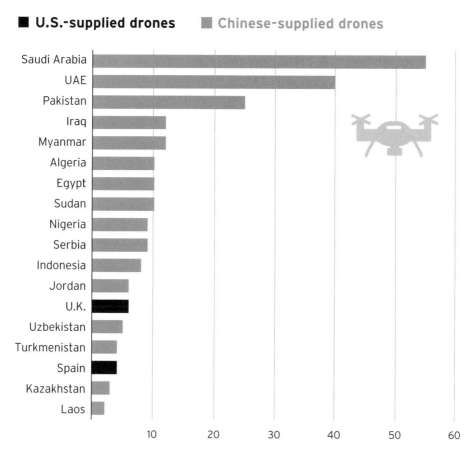

Source: Stockholm International Peace Research Institute via Bloomberg.

Does Our Budget Allocation Align With Our Threats?

America's giant defense budget still wasn't enough to protect against its greatest threat in recent history—which came not from tanks and bombs but from an enemy one four-hundredth the width of a human hair. The CDC had roughly 1% of the defense budget to respond to a pandemic that's killed more Americans than all of our twentieth-century wars combined. From Warren Buffet to Jeff Bezos, the greatest investors and CEOs are the greatest allocators of capital, deploying it to seize opportunities, ensure long-term growth, and minimize risks. The same applies to governments. The U.S. government is one of the largest managers of capital in the world. And it has underinvested in the institutions that serve as the connective tissue holding the nation together.

72

U.S. Department of Defense Budget vs. Centers for Disease Control Budget

FY 2021

$704B
Department
of Defense

$7.9B CDC

Centers for Disease Control

Sources: CDC, Defense.gov.

Erosion of the World's Most Important Brand

The U.S. has long been a global role model. Building and maintaining a reputation for leadership in the promotion of democracy and freedom has been a bedrock component of American foreign policy since long before President Truman put rhetoric into action with the Marshall Plan. Even Ronald Reagan—especially Ronald Reagan—understood that the fist of power was most effective when it was wielded by a hero, not a villain. In 1985, he declared it America's "mission" to "nourish and defend freedom and democracy," and he made democracy promotion central to American diplomacy and foreign aid—which he increased more than any prior Republican president.

In 2000, international sentiments toward the U.S. were strong. Roughly 8 in every 10 British citizens had a favorable view of the U.S. This statistic was consistent in Germany, Italy, and halfway across the globe, in Japan. But U.S. foreign policy and domestic strife have undermined that brand equity. In 2020, the citizens of most countries saw America in a dramatically less favorable light. Many felt that American democracy itself had fallen behind: For roughly every 10 citizens in developed nations, 6 believe that the U.S. used to be a good example of democracy but no longer is.

73

Share of Population With a Favorable View of the U.S.

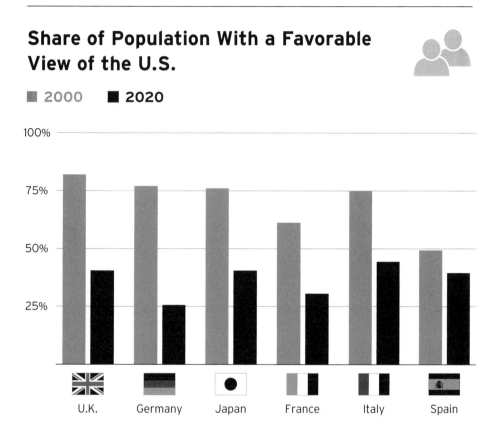

■ 2000 ■ 2020

Source: Pew Research Center.

The U.S. Is No Longer the World's Laboratory

America's superpower has always been its optimism, and an optimistic nation invests in the future. In 1960, the U.S. was the largest spender on R&D, accounting for 69% of global spending. That money ensured the U.S. was a global leader in science and technology, providing us with weather satellites, GPS, the internet, drones, and most recently, messenger-RNA vaccines. Such vaccines were unproven until the U.S. government granted Moderna $25 million in 2013. Almost a decade and a half-billion doses later, it's safe to say the investment paid off. The U.S. is spending more than ever on R&D, but it now accounts for only 30% of global investment, as other nations recognize the competitive advantages good research brings.

74

U.S. Share of Global R&D Spending

■ **U.S.**   ■ **Rest of world**

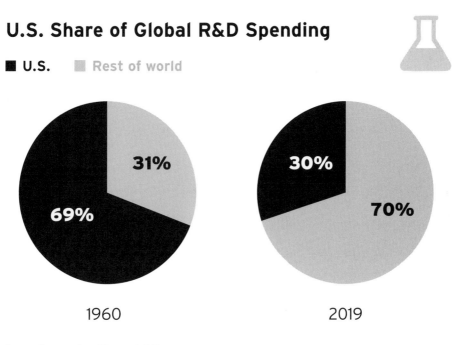

1960

2019

Source: Congressional Research Office.

Note: Includes public and private R&D expenditures.

Clean Energy's Silk Road Runs Through China

Many companies wrap themselves in the flag of climate change. Much of that may be corporate yogababble, but it helps position them under the huge addressable market of clean energy and the potential for the outsized valuations it brings. And there's no doubt that vast sums will be poured into the development of clean tech in the next few decades.

However, one of the dirty little secrets of the green revolution is that it requires some very grubby mineral extraction. Rare earth metals, cobalt, lithium, and other minerals are essential to batteries, magnets, and other advanced industrial applications. If the future of tech is green, it's also red. Few clean energy minerals are produced or processed on American soil. Another country dominates the extraction and processing of these essential materials: China.

75

Clean Energy Mineral Refinement and Processing by Country

2010-2020

■ U.S. **⊡ China** **■ Indonesia** **▨ Chile** **□ Japan** **▧ Other**

	Refined	Processed

Copper

Nickel

Cobalt

Rare earths

Lithium

50%   100%   50%   100%

Source: IEA.

The Spawning Ground for Capitalism's Apex Predators

America's innovative spirit and celebration of entrepreneurship have helped it long dominate the rankings of the largest 50 companies as measured by market capitalization. Our share of those companies has grown from 30 to 32 in the past three decades. The most impressive growth in representation, though, has come from China, which went from having 0 members to 8 over the same period. This largely came at the expense of Europe, which lost more representatives in the top 50 than any other region. China has also seen a rapid increase in the number of wealthy individuals. As of 2021, the country had 626 billionaires, more than twice the total of 2020, and nearly as many members of the three-comma club as the U.S., which recorded 724.

76

Top 50 Global Companies by Nationality

By market value

■ U.S.   ⊞ China   ■ EMEA   ▨ Other APAC   ▧ Other Americas

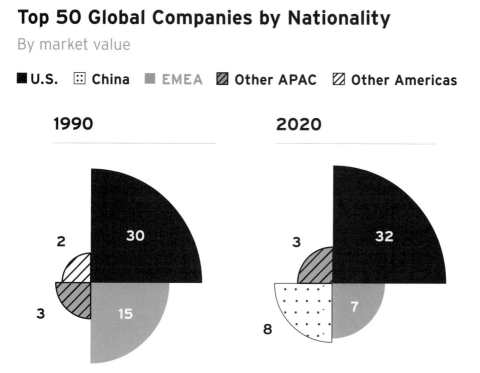

1990

2
30
3
15

2020

3
32
8
7

Source: Bloomberg.

CHAPTER 8

The Bright Side of Instability

The terrible thing about crises is that they always happen. The wonderful thing is that they always end.

Life is change. The capacity to grow and evolve is what separates living things from mere objects. Stasis is death, to an organism and to a society. A healthy society is vibrant and dynamic, generating ideas and innovation in every field.

Change opens doors for young people, immigrants, and other newcomers to industries and organizations. For the first forty years of my life, there wasn't a single new, independent automobile brand. As long as cars were powered by gasoline and sold through franchise dealers, that wasn't going to change. But then a generation of innovators developed the technology necessary to build a car that runs on electricity; now I'm driving a Tesla, have a deposit down on a Rivian, and I'm eyeing a Lucid.

The first chapter of this book was about change, and while much of the rest has been devoted to chronicling the ways those changes have hurt us, there was real upside to the dynamism unleashed in the 1980s.

For example, on December 31, 1983, there was only one telephone company of any note in the U.S., just one company that essentially controlled all electronic communications: AT&T. On January 1, 1984—thanks to a decade of work by the Department of Justice's antitrust division—there were eight: AT&T offered long-distance, and seven former subsidiaries handled local calls in their regions. These newly independent companies immediately started competing for business. Sprint and MCI, which had been nibbling at the edges of telecom for years, remade the long-distance business as a competitive, innovative field. Competition encouraged AT&T to ramp up its R&D budget by 30% in just five years, despite divestiture slashing its revenue in half. By the 1990s, cable television companies and new entrants were all investing billions in the advanced networks that would carry us into the internet era.

Capitalism is rife with failure, and that's one of its best features. When a restaurant goes out of business, the pain of that loss must be balanced against the opening it gives a new chef, who can finally get a lease to bring something better to the neighborhood. A decline in apartment rents means young people can move to the city and bring their energy and ideas to a larger market.

Change always entails risk, because in a dynamic economy accumulated capital can be lost. So it's natural for winners to want to arrest the pace of change, to shift from offense to defense once the score is in their favor. But doing this is short-sighted and detrimental to the long-term health of society. Let the gale of creative destruction blow.

Crises Trigger Growth

Human history is a history of crises. The challenges we face today highlight how much we stand to lose. There have been far darker times, but light always returns. When it does, it illuminates new opportunities, paths forward once barred by entrenched interests or outdated thinking.

This has held true even in some of humanity's worst moments. The Black Plague, a bubonic epidemic in fourteenth-century Europe, killed more than 25 million people—at least *one-third* the population—in just four years. But even the Black Plague had a silver lining. The reduced population led to a higher per-capita income and a shift toward urban living, which created an outsized demand for discretionary urban products. This forced cities to grow in size, and eventually tuned up Europe's long dormant economic engine, which would sputter to life over the next century. The authors of a study of this phenomenon dubbed plague, war, and urbanization "the three horsemen of riches," because they jump-start urban growth and economic activity over the long term.

77

Effect of the Black Death on European Urbanization Rates

Population indexed to the year 1000

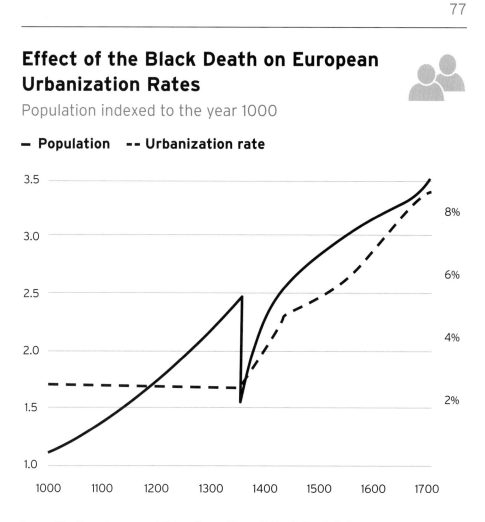

— **Population**   -- **Urbanization rate**

Source: "The Three Horsemen of Riches: Plague, War, and Urbanization in Early Modern Europe," Voigtländer and Voth, November 2009.

Note: Population and urbanization numbers are estimates.

Resetting Expectations

There is no better time to enter the workforce than in a recession. Economic instability forces us to recalibrate our expectations about the future and be more inquisitive about where real value lies. These are tremendous outlooks for young people to adopt, which helps to explain why recessionary environments increase job satisfaction among new workers across the board. A study by Emily Bianchi of Goizueta Business School showed that graduating amid average conditions vs. the best economic conditions causes a 10% increase in job satisfaction. Graduating in the worst vs. the best economic conditions correlates with a 25% increase. With greater job satisfaction comes more motivation in the workplace, leading to increased productivity and higher pay.

78

Effect of Graduating in the Worst vs. the Best Economic Conditions

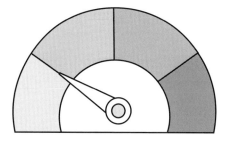

+25%

Increase in job satisfaction

Source: "The Bright Side of Bad Times: The Affective Advantages of Entering the Workforce in a Recession," Bianchi, October 2013.

Surging Startups

There were 5.4 million new business applications in 2021. That's 23% higher than 2020's record 4.4 million, and 35% higher than the total in 2019. While pandemic economics haven't resulted in a garden-variety recession—in either its duration (short) or its recovery (K-shaped)—there are factors that have made this period the best time to start a business in a decade.

The combination of historic savings, government stimulus, and record asset appreciation shaped a wave of consumer spending unlike anything we've seen since baby boomers first decided consumerism was a virtue. A gestalt grew among consumers and enterprises to question the status quo and be open to new products and services. And innovative fields emerged to disrupt traditional industries, just as viral immunity kicked in for most Americans.

Of course, applications are a forward-looking indicator—they're only a proxy for actual business creation—and not all of these applications result in a full-fledged business. Still, they serve as a marker for optimism.

79

Number of Business Applications

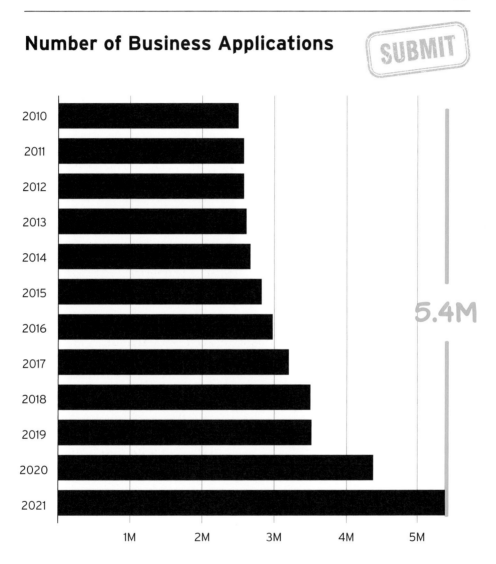

SUBMIT

Source: U.S. Census Bureau's Business Formation Statistics.

Immigrants Are the Original Entrepreneurs

We are in a boom time of new business formation, and many would never have begun but for 1) a global pandemic, and 2) the incredible work of (you guessed it) immigrants.

Over the past thirty years, immigrants to the U.S. have started businesses at greater rates than American-born citizens. In 2020, the rate of new entrepreneurs among immigrants was 0.59%, nearly double the rate among those born in the U.S. Some of the most important companies in tech were founded or cofounded by immigrants, including Google, eBay, PayPal, and Tesla.

And it makes sense: if you're an immigrant who took a chance on a new country, you might be more willing to take a risk on a new business, too. From labor to entrepreneurship, immigrants are the lifeblood of our economy. We would miss opportunities if we fail to attract and retain them.

80

Share of Adults Who Started Their First Business

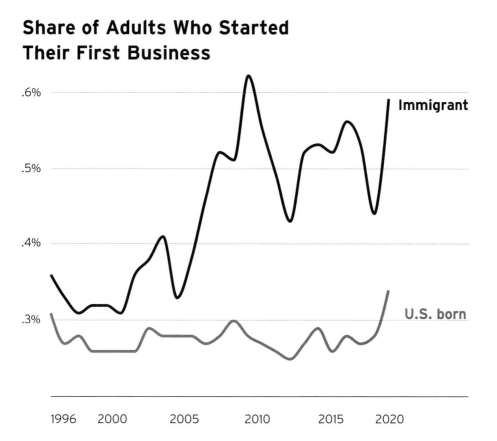

Source: Kauffman Foundation.

Seeking Refuge

It's great to have freedom from worry. We Americans take a lot of this type of freedom for granted. Refugees flee their homelands with an infant on their back and toddler at their side to experience that.

Despite the challenges waiting for them in the U.S., refugees show an astounding level of upward mobility. In the first five years after refugees settle here, their median household income is just shy of $22,000. But as their time in America stretches on and their opportunities expand, so does their take-home pay. After living here for more than twenty-five years, the median household income for refugees reaches $67,000 on average—notably higher than that of the population overall, at $53,000.

81

Growth of Median Refugee Household Income

By number of years in the U.S.

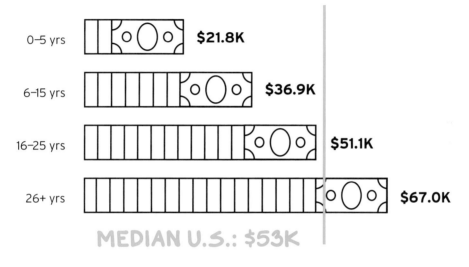

0–5 yrs   **$21.8K**

6–15 yrs   **$36.9K**

16–25 yrs   **$51.1K**

26+ yrs   **$67.0K**

MEDIAN U.S.: $53K

Source: New American Economy; American Community Survey, 2011 – 2015.

Getting Banked

Unequal access to banking is a global problem. Almost a third of the world's adults, 1.7 billion, are unbanked. In Colombia, Nigeria, Pakistan, and a few other countries, more than 50% of adults are unbanked. In the United States, it's 5.4%, or 7.1 million households. This is more than an economic issue—it's a societal problem. When people are excluded from financial institutions, they're excluded from the fabric of the community.

For banking innovators, this is an opportunity. Take Argentine fintech Ualá. In just four years, more than 4 million people—about 9% of the country—have opened an account with the company, and more than 25% of eighteen- to twenty-five-year-olds now have a tarjeta Ualá, an online wallet.

There's immense value creation for multiple stakeholders in this space. Financial inclusion bolsters the middle class and forms a solid base for democracy.

82

Economies With Half or More of Adults Unbanked

2017

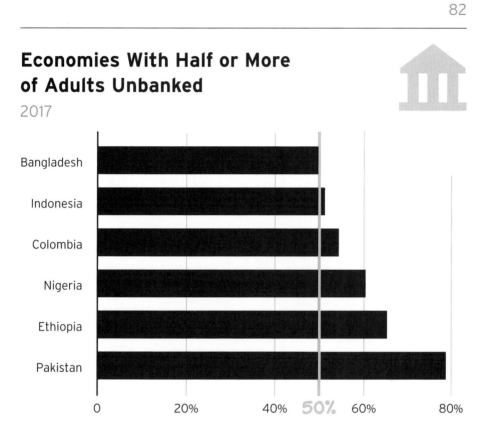

Source: Global Findex Database.

CHAPTER 9

Possible Futures

The best way to predict the future is to make it.

Where we are headed doesn't depend on the conductivity of silicon or the depth of Arctic sea ice. It depends on us, and what we do tomorrow and the next day. What's singular about this moment is the scope of possibility. America is more populous, powerful, and connected than ever. The range of potential consequences of our actions is as open-ended today as it has been since at least 1980, or possibly 1945.

The changes wrought by social media feel momentous, but we're only a little more than a decade into living online. The accelerating pace of change may work *for* us as well as against us. In the late 1990s, Microsoft was a colossus, the AT&T of its era. And it was notorious for using its power to suppress competition and restrict any innovation it couldn't control. A tech magazine ran a cover featuring Bill Gates as a member of *Star Trek: The Next Generation*'s Borg—"Resistance is futile ... you will be assimilated"—and the image became one of the internet's first memes. His company fended off a major antitrust lawsuit from the government, but even so, its dominance didn't persist. Within just a few years, after the resurgence of Apple, the rise of Google, and the emergence of a dozen other new powers, it was clear that Microsoft, while still a titan, was to be one of many.

Trends can change direction with surprising speed, and no matter what course an economy or culture appears to set, more often than not we end up somewhere else. This chapter proposes possible futures as seen through varying lenses of technology, economics, and policy. As with any good prediction, the value in ours lies in the conversations they catalyze.

Printing Our Way to Prosperity

The government typically pays for things with money it obtains either by raising taxes or borrowing. But the government has another, unique way to generate funds: It can print more money. In practice, this involves bond sales and accounting sleight of hand, not a printing press, but the end result is the same: money for nothing.

Fears that increasing the money supply will lead to inflation have traditionally kept governments from employing this approach aggressively. But some economists think that fear is unjustified and say that governments should be more willing to print money. When combined with a government job guarantee and other measures, this philosophy is known as "modern monetary theory." Ideally, the new money fuels productive economic activity, which creates value sufficient to absorb the additional currency, holding off inflation.

Crisis encourages innovation, and in recent decades, the U.S. government has twice resorted to aggressively expanding the money supply—after the 2008 financial crisis and the Covid-19 pandemic. In the short run, it appears to have worked—the Covid recession was shorter and shallower than anyone predicted. But the recovery has also been accompanied by inflation.

Creating money is a hard habit for a government to break. It's likely that this won't be Uncle Sam's last trip to the money dealer. A willingness to pour money into the economy might produce the rising tide of income that lifts all our boats.

83

Money Supply

M2 money stock

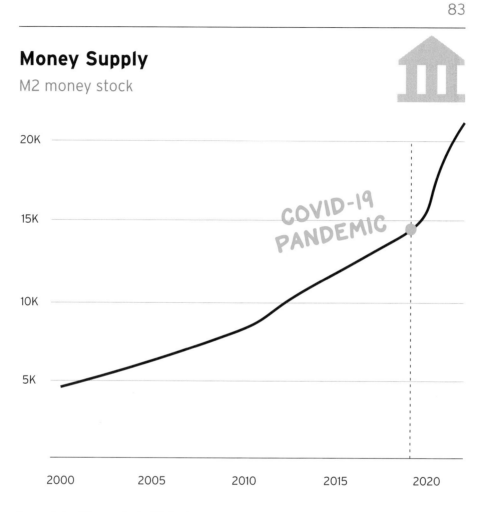

COVID-19
PANDEMIC

20K

15K

10K

5K

2000   2005   2010   2015   2020

Source: Federal Reserve Bank of St. Louis.

Note: M2 is the Federal Reserve's main measure of the U.S. money supply and includes liquid currency (M1) plus savings deposits under $100,000 and shares in retail money market mutual funds.

Drowning in Cash

One of the specters that haunts economics is hyperinflation. Central bankers' nightmares feature grainy black-and-white photos of women carting wheelbarrows full of cash through the streets of Weimar Germany to buy bread. Runaway inflation arises from a confluence of factors, but the most notorious culprit is a government that prints too much money. Loading up the money supply devalues the currency, requiring the government to print even more, further devaluing the currency, etc. In Germany after World War I, prices rose so fast that restaurants stopped printing menus—they went out of date between the appetizer and dessert.

Could it happen here? The U.S. government spent its way out of the Covid recession, making an unprecedented injection of money into the economy. It worked, but printing cash to solve problems is a hard habit to break. And by late 2021 it was clear that inflation was on the rise. A little inflation isn't such a bad thing; for debtors, it has a bright side—when money is worth less, debts are, too. But hyperinflation destroys economies.

It may be that modern economies are not subject to this risk in the same way early industrial societies were. And certainly, our political climate, as bad as it might feel, is nothing like that of 1920s Germany. At that time, Germany saw hundreds of political assassinations and occupation by the French military, which was seeking reparations payments. But "this time is different" are famous last words.

84

Hyperinflation in Weimar Germany

Annualized rate of inflation, log scale

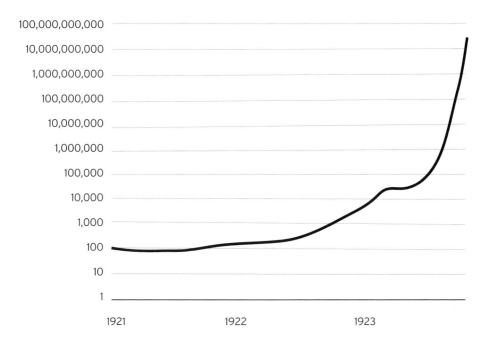

Source: *Financial Times*.

Investment in the Social Safety Net

For most of my life, a dividing line in American politics has been drawn through government provision of social services. The left wanted to spend more, the right to spend less. But in the aftermath of the 2008 financial crisis, with the rise of right-wing populism, and now Covid, there are signs of an increased willingness to invest in the commonwealth.

Of course, political partisanship hampers this, because neither party wants to give the other a win. Democrats were in no hurry to let President Trump's "Infrastructure Week" ever become a reality. After his loss in 2020, the Republicans suddenly remembered their commitment to fiscal responsibility and voted against an actual infrastructure bill. But stimulus checks were (unsurprisingly) popular, as is the expansion of the child tax credit. For all the political heat it continues to generate, Obamacare is also popular, and its actual provisions even more so when polltakers leave out the brand name. Social spending has ticked up in recent years, though the U.S. is still well behind Western European nations, which spend 20% to 30% of GDP on their citizens.

For the first time in my memory, we might have the political raw material necessary to mend our fraying social safety net. Done effectively, investments in early education, protections against job losses, and care for the sick, disabled, and elderly can be economic superchargers. Risk is at the heart of capitalist achievement, and we are understandably more risk averse when a failed enterprise would mean losing our home or healthcare for our family.

85

Public Social Spending as a Share of GDP

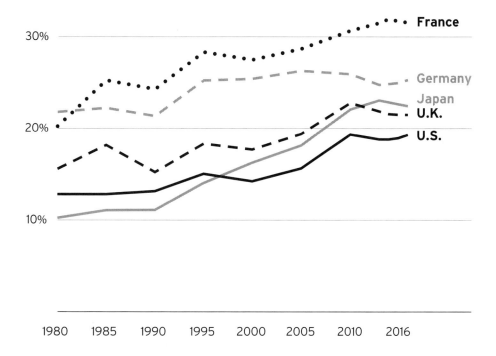

30%

France

Germany

Japan

U.K.

U.S.

20%

10%

1980 1985 1990 1995 2000 2005 2010 2016

Source: OECD via Our World in Data.

Smothered by the Safety Net

Social spending can protect the vulnerable from the sharp edges of capitalism, and it lifts us all by building a more just society. That's the argument, anyway. The downside is that it can mire the government in debt, create ineffective administrative zombies that are insulated from market forces, and worst of all, snuff out the spark of innovation. The European commitment to social spending can't be ignored when considering that between 1980 and 2020, the U.S. economy has grown faster than Europe's in twenty-eight of the past forty-one years.

To be clear, I am not someone who believes that workers are only productive when they fear starvation. That's immoral and simply wrong. Economic anxiety is like high blood pressure: it's a drag on energy and effectiveness, not a spur. Only someone who's never been poor thinks poor people work harder when we take more away from them.

But to work, social spending has to be done effectively, not squandered on bureaucracy. It has to be delivered in the context of a society where mobility remains possible, and where risk is still rewarded.

86

Difference in Annual GDP Growth Rate

U.S. minus Europe

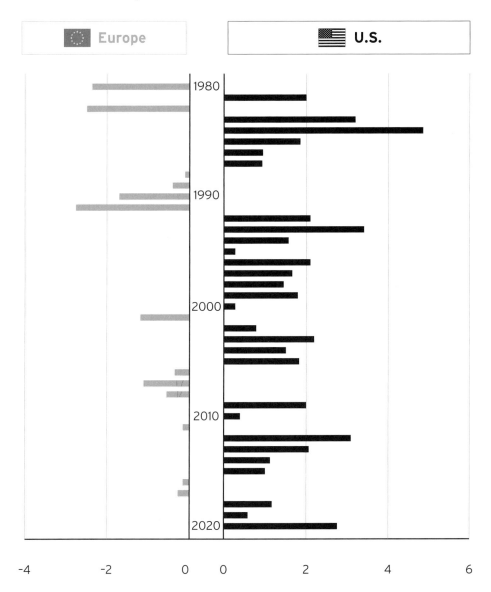

Metadystopia

Global megacorporations don't often change their names, so when
Facebook renamed itself Meta, that was a strong signal the tech
community is serious about the metaverse. It wants to build an economic
and social world comprised entirely of bits. And why not? Big Tech's
future profits won't come from besting the competition—they have none.
Their opportunity will come from stealing away the precious few hours a
day we don't spend in front of a screen. Yet. So they're promoting a future
where we are never offline.

I'm a skeptic. A lot of the hype is predicated on virtual reality, which is
one of the great snipe hunts, a technology that's always just about to get
real. Access issues aside, does anyone besides our tech overlords think
living on the internet full time is a good idea? Rage- and fear-inducing
content, fake news, pyramid schemes, phishing attacks, and trackers
following our every move. At least now this world is limited by the four
corners of our devices. The Chinese government is spending billions to
monitor every moment of its citizens' days. In a metaverse future, we're
going to buy our own surveillance devices and pay $14.99 a month for the
privilege of being spied on.

But there is one reason for optimism: Children growing up today are
metaverse natives. They're building things and making friends on
Minecraft and Roblox, and are using other platforms I haven't even heard
of. Perhaps that experience will give them the wherewithal to build out a
metaverse that sucks less than this -verse. We'll see.

87

Estimated Active Monthly Roblox and Minecraft Users

■ R**Q**BL**Q**X   ■ MINECRAFT

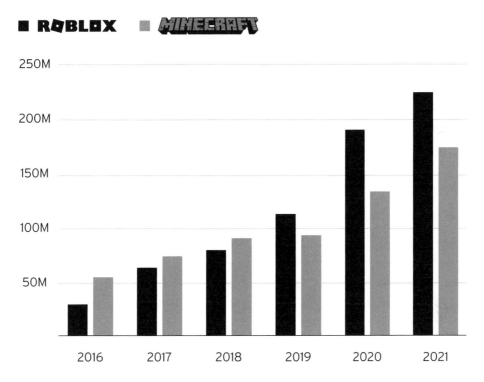

Sources: Backlinko, Activeplayer.io, Statista.

Fast Future

Covid acted as an accelerant on existing trends with a common theme: dispersion. The connective power of technology has the ironic effect of allowing us to be farther apart. Managed well, this Great Dispersion can be an unlock, a way of reorganizing our resources more efficiently.

For workers in bit-based jobs, it means access to employment globally. Office space will be reconfigured to focus on meaningful interactions and to give companies the flexibility to build out teams without regard for geography. And more jobs will be bit-based: Healthcare will see a radical shift toward remote access, making more efficient use of scarce skills and bringing care to underserved regions. Educational institutions where physical space limits enrollment can double or triple class sizes, rotating students through on-campus and dispersed phases and opening satellite locations.

Bits can't be uncoupled from atoms, and we'll maximize this unlock with investment in transportation: fast-moving people at every scale, from cross-continent supersonic to crosstown underground; fast-moving goods to doorsteps, not warehouses.

88

Percentage of U.S. Work Teams That Plan to Work Remotely in 2025

Compared to pre-pandemic

■ **Fully remote**　　■ **Partially remote**　　■ Not remote

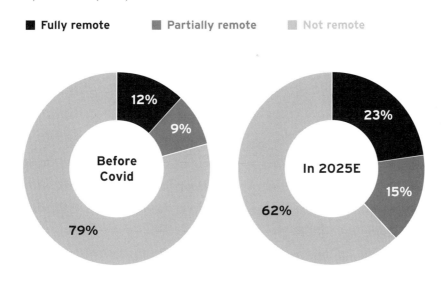

Source: Survey conducted October 21 – November 7, 2020, via Upwork/Statista.

Space Is Lonely Without Friends

The dispersion Covid triggered has a dark side, and it will dominate without the right investments. Cutting people off from human contact— whether at our jobs, in our recreation, or even while doing simple tasks like grocery shopping—puts us at risk of digging deeper into our silos. We learn tolerance through exposure, not isolation, and the connective tissue of the commonwealth doesn't grow well over Wi-Fi.

Tethered all our waking hours to our devices, we've become subject to the manipulations of those who control the pipes, and their track record for enlightened despotism isn't good. We're anxious, overstressed, and hunched over our laptops. Friendship is dwindling—people report fewer close friends than they did thirty years ago, and 15% of men and 10% of women have no close friends at all. Our public and shared spaces risk decay—or privatization to become playgrounds for the wealthiest few.

The most affluent, the billionaire class whose innovations are giving us this work/live/play-from-home dystopia, will be a million miles away. Literally. They're taking their windfall profits and investing in moon bases and Mars retreats. I don't think their vision will ever be realized— Mars is a freezing, airless, irradiated rock. But our billionaire class is arrogant enough to burn off the prosperity of our age in a futile attempt to conquer the next one.

89

Decline in Friendship

Percentage who report having the following number of close friends, not counting their relatives

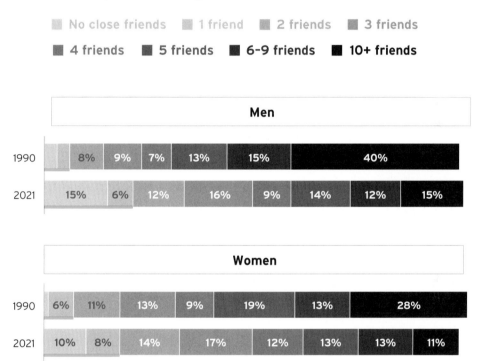

Legend: No close friends · 1 friend · 2 friends · 3 friends · 4 friends · 5 friends · 6-9 friends · 10+ friends

Men

1990: 8% | 9% | 7% | 13% | 15% | 40%

2021: 15% | 6% | 12% | 16% | 9% | 14% | 12% | 15%

Women

1990: 6% | 11% | 13% | 9% | 19% | 13% | 28%

2021: 10% | 8% | 14% | 17% | 12% | 13% | 13% | 11%

Sources: American Perspectives Survey, May 2021; Gallup 1990.

Note: Figure may not add up to 100% due to rounding.

CHAPTER 10

What We Must Do

All anyone can ask for is a level playing field,
a fair start, and the security needed to take risks.

I'm sometimes criticized for focusing on the problems of tech or business or society, and not proposing solutions. Well, guilty as charged, I suppose. But let me say two things.

First, these problems flow in part from failures of perception and awareness. My cohort of economically successful people vastly overestimates our own contribution to our success. Society has been telling us that our nice homes and fancy cars must mean we're hard-working geniuses, and why should we argue the point? The flip side is also true. Society tells those who've been dealt a bad hand, who've never caught a break, that their failure must come from a lack of grit, an incapacity to dream big. I believe that just pulling the veil of hype that's been laid across our unequal society is part of the solution to that inequality. While there are bad apples, in my experience people are mostly good, and they want to do right by their society. We're more often wrong than bad, but the result is the same. America is a country of great wealth and achievement, yet a chronic illness can bankrupt a family. So my aim is to reset our assessment of what got us here, with the hope that a clearer perspective can help alter where we're headed.

Second, to be blunt, things are really fucking bad. The dashboard of threats, from inflated asset values to irreversible climate change to armed assaults on government proceedings, is flashing red and getting worse. If I spent my entire public life pointing out the risks we face, I would never run out of material.

That said, there is also a lot that is going right, and a lot that is promising, and my critics have a point. In his first inaugural address, President Clinton famously said, "There is nothing wrong with America that cannot be cured by what is right with America." Those are words that would have fit Reagan's 1981 speech about the "business of America." For that matter, they would have suited Lincoln speaking to a broken union, or FDR during the Depression. They are words I deeply believe in today.

Moreover, it matters that we "cure" America. That belief has been implicit throughout this book, but I want to make it explicit here. Although it's out of fashion, I remain an American Exceptionalist. This country really is different, in ways that make it, in words used by presidents too numerous to list, "a city on a hill," a beacon for the optimistic and the innovative. That's not to say I think America is perfect—I doubt anyone could get this far in the book and think that's my view—but as a nation born not of ethnicity or dynastic conquest but rather built on the foundation of an ideal, it holds a special promise. It remains a promise unfulfilled, but one I believe is within our grasp.

We've gotten closest to realizing our ideals when we've balanced ruthless capitalism with the ballast of a strong middle class. Our drift away from that course is at the heart of this book. Shifting us back is the objective of my recommendations.

Simplify the Tax Code

The idea of simplifying the tax system might be the only policy that all Americans universally support. Yet the tax code only gets more and more complex. In 1955, the Internal Revenue Code stood at 409,000 words; today it has roughly 4 million.

The complexity of the code is, in and of itself, a tax on the poor. The wealthy employ small militias to conquer the system and minimize their taxes. The dodges that benefit the wealthy are unavailable to everyday Americans, as is the high-priced advice necessary to take advantage of them. What this complexity means for regular people is a huge loss of time. In 2012, the IRS's National Taxpayer Advocate estimated it took a total 6.1 billion hours for all taxpayers to handle their taxes. Compare that to the filer's experience in thirty-six countries, including Germany, Japan, Norway, and Sweden, where the government calculates taxes and provides taxpayers with a pre-filled return.

We should revise the tax code with uniform definitions and eliminate itemized deductions in favor of higher standard deductions for households. Tax savings programs from Roth IRAs to Coverdell education savings accounts should also be consolidated to achieve one simple goal: encouraging personal savings by avoiding double taxation of them. And we should end the favorable tax treatment given to income earned by the sale of assets. Money (and the money it makes) is not more noble than sweat.

90

Words in the Tax Code

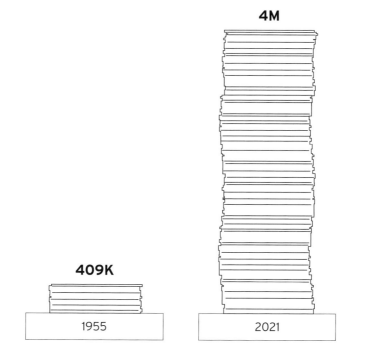

4M

409K

1955

2021

Sources: IRS, Tax Foundation, National Taypayers' Union.

Rebuild the Regulatory System

Our regulatory systems are underfunded, and the regulators are outnumbered by those protecting the industries that have a stranglehold on consumer spending and activity. Thus, we're left with inefficient systems protecting workers and families.

To fix this, we must reinvest in fair, efficient enforcement to prevent monopolies from suppressing innovation and competition, and instead provide security and resilience for individuals and small companies.

Amazon and Facebook, two companies on the DOJ and FTC's beat, spent roughly $18 million and $20 million, respectively, on lobbying in 2020. Amazon has been increasing its spending in this category at a rapid pace—it's up 460% since 2012. Amazon has more full-time lobbyists than there are sitting U.S. senators.

It's not just Big Tech. Big Oil spends millions of dollars to slap green paint over the climate implications of its practices. BP, Chevron, ExxonMobil, and Shell have collectively spent $374.7 million on federal lobbying since 2011. Meanwhile, the Environmental Protection Agency's enforcement funding and head count have been in decline since 2006. We must reinvest in regulatory bodies, not least those that protect our shared environment.

91

EPA Enforcement Budget and Staffing

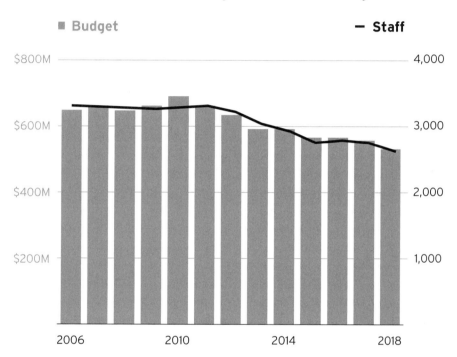

Source: EPA.

Restore the Algebra of Deterrence

Regulations only work when the profits from engaging in a wrongful activity are less than the punishment times the chance of getting caught. For Big Tech, the math isn't even close. The FTC made headlines for smacking Facebook with a record-breaking $5 billion fine in 2019 for consumer privacy violations, but that represented just 7% of the company's year-end revenue.

Sure, the company got caught ... but it doesn't matter. Record fines amount to weeks of cash flow. All the FTC did was create an illusion of enforcement. Nothing will change until someone is arrested and charged.

Think about it: Would Michael Milken have been sentenced to ten years in federal prison in 2021? Likely not if we're basing that outcome on the government action handed down to Mark Zuckerberg. He continues to smear lipstick over the cancer that is Facebook, and until we see a financial disincentive for his relentless systemic misconduct, we'll continue to see no more than a Band-Aid put on the crises his company creates.

92

FTC Facebook Fine Relative to Market Cap and Revenue

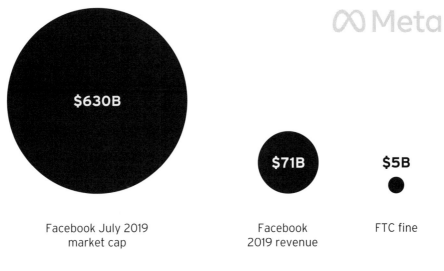

Facebook July 2019
market cap

Facebook
2019 revenue

FTC fine

Sources: Seeking Alpha, The Federal Trade Commission,
and Facebook.

Reform Section 230

Social media companies have largely been immunized from scrutiny because of a law that was passed in 1996—when just 16% of Americans had access to the internet via a computer tethered to a phone cord. Facebook, Twitter, and YouTube didn't yet exist, and Amazon was an online bookseller.

Today, more than half of the world's population uses social media, and though this expansion has produced enormous stakeholder value, the externalities have grown faster than the revenue. Social media users are exposed to algorithms of enragement—fostering an ecosystem of contempt, partisanship, and polarization. Our teens are depressed and suffering from device addiction.

Social media companies no longer need special treatment. They now have the resources and reach to play by the same rules as every other media company—rules that make the penalty and likelihood of being caught greater than the upside of ransacking democracy. These rules justly shift the cost of externalities from the commonwealth to the companies that create them.

93

A Timeline of Social Media Companies Since Section 230's Passage

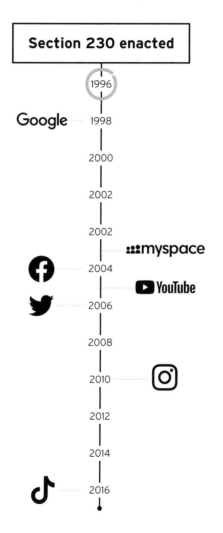

Source: Prof G analysis.

Rethink the Land of the ~~Free~~ Incarcerated

The U.S. leads the world in many things that elicit pride, but incarceration is not one of them. As of 2021, 629 out of every 100,000 Americans were behind bars, the highest rate of incarceration of any country in the world. Cuba, an authoritarian regime that imprisons people for "pre-criminal social dangerousness," has a lower percentage of its people in jails. America's incarceration rate is twice as high as Russia's, not to mention seventeen times higher than Japan's. If the U.S. prison population were a city, it would be the fifth-largest in the nation—more populated than Atlanta, Miami, Cincinnati, and Memphis combined. Black and Hispanic people make up almost 60% of the prison population, despite accounting for roughly a third of the U.S. population. And all those prisons cost more than $80 billion per year to maintain.

We must rethink this. Sentencing for nonviolent offenses should be re-evaluated, and prisoners with no history of violence should be considered for release. Drug courts, diversion programs, and other alternatives to prison should be expanded. Prison release should be accompanied by re-entry programs and education. Locking a young man away for a youthful mistake that harmed nobody and then dumping him on the street without any preparation years later merely compounds the problem. We broke criminal justice, and we need to fix it.

94

Incarceration Rates

Per 100,000 people, August 2021

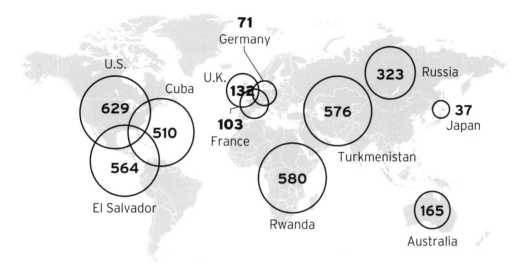

Source: World Prison Brief.

Enact a One-Time Wealth Tax

One of the largest transfers of wealth from the young to the old in U.S. history came with the government response to the Covid pandemic. It issued a massive $5 trillion in stimulus, and essentially $3 trillion ended up in the hands of the wrong people. That amount could have been $30,000 for every American who reported pandemic wage losses. Huge swaths of America suffered, while the rich got richer.

That $30,000 in the hands of those who needed it the most would have gone much further toward repairing the economy, as more money would have ended up in the economy rather than in the markets. And who better to determine which businesses deserve to survive and are prepared for a new economy than consumers?

In the future, stimulus packages should be limited to supporting people who are food and housing insecure—not Delta Air Lines or your neighbor who owns seven dry cleaners.

But since we're already $3 trillion in the hole, we need to recover some of those losses. We should impose a one-time wealth tax. A 2% tax on the richest 5% of households would raise up to $1 trillion. (The initial stock market bump triggered by the CARES Act's passage helped the richest American stock owners accrue an additional $2 trillion.)

If we don't align financial rewards and penalties with the health of our commonwealth and its citizenry, we are doomed to a pattern of failed responses to crises.

95

Covid Relief Spending

$3 trillion	What we could have done
• Paycheck Protection Program • Tax breaks • Other handouts to the wealthy	**$30K** to every single one of the **100M Americans** who reported **pandemic-related wage losses** in 2020

Sources: appropriations.house.gov, bls.gov.

Rebrand Nuclear

Nuclear energy suffers from a tragic branding problem. The technology is a carbon-free and reliable source of twenty-four-hour-per-day power. A single generator produces enough electricity to run all the homes in Philadelphia. And nuclear power has been in wide use around the world for generations.

Yet only 29% of Americans view it favorably, and 49% view it unfavorably, making it the most unpopular energy source after coal. Our apprehension toward this powerful clean energy source stems from isolated, highly infrequent incidents. In reality, nuclear power is one of the safest energy sources in the world, registering accident- and pollution-related death rates roughly 300 times lower than those of coal and oil, relative to their energy production.

It's time for a rebrand.

96

Death Rates and Emissions from Energy Production

Deaths per terawatt-hour of energy production

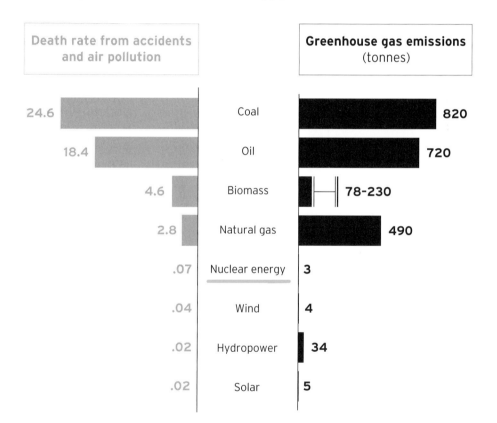

Death rate from accidents and air pollution		Greenhouse gas emissions (tonnes)
24.6	Coal	820
18.4	Oil	720
4.6	Biomass	78-230
2.8	Natural gas	490
.07	Nuclear energy	3
.04	Wind	4
.02	Hydropower	34
.02	Solar	5

Sources: Markandya & Wilkinson (2007) and Sovacool et al. (2016) via Our World in Data.

Support Children and Family Formation

In 2019, nearly 1 in 7 American children lived in poverty. We are the richest nation in human history. Letting this continue is beyond unacceptable: it's bad policy. Giving every child a solid start in the world—food, shelter, education, and hope—is the best investment we can make in our future. Argue with me all you want about the minimum wage or antitrust enforcement or Tesla's share price. Early education and good childcare leads to prosperous economic outcomes for *everyone*. Today's children will be the workers, thinkers, and leaders of tomorrow.

After the District of Columbia implemented universal preschool in 2008, maternal labor force participation climbed steadily from 65% to 76% in 2016. Furthermore, a 2011 study by Harvard economist Raj Chetty and his colleagues found that students who were randomly assigned to higher-quality classrooms in grades K–3 were more likely to attend college, save more for retirement, earn higher incomes, and live in better neighborhoods as adults. Let's make sure Professor Chetty can't continue his research—make *all* classrooms high quality. I doubt he'll mind.

The simplest way to aid children is also one of the most effective: give the parents money. The federal child tax credit currently gives up to $2,000 per child to middle-income households. That's nowhere near sufficient. A universal $3,000-per-child allowance would almost halve child poverty and racial inequities. Even critics, who are concerned that the credit would encourage some recipients not to work, acknowledge that it would do more than any current program to reduce child poverty.

97

Child Tax Credit's Impact on Child Poverty Rates

2019

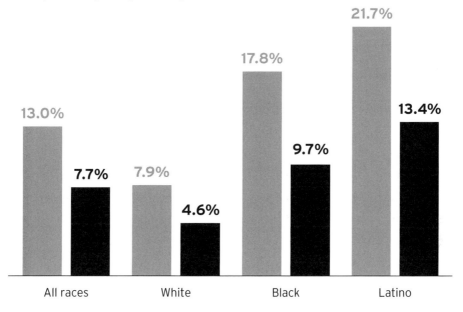

■ Existing policy ($2K-per-child allowance)

■ Expanded policy ($3K-per-child allowance)

Source: Center on Budget and Policy Priorities.

Reform Higher Ed

Higher education needs incentives to drive the expansion of seats. The best incentive? Money. One proposed solution is to cancel over $1.5 trillion in student debt, but that would only reinforce higher education's model of exploitative costs, at a huge expense to taxpayers. Instead, we should target the almost $600 billion in endowments held by U.S. colleges on a tax-free basis.

Elite colleges have become hedge funds masquerading as educators, so they should be taxed as the former. A simple requirement for maintaining tax exemption on an endowment: Colleges should expand freshman seats faster than the population is growing. That's for the elites, with massive endowments. For the majority of schools, which educate the vast majority of students, we need a grand bargain. Public subsidies and state funding should be increased, but directly linked to the same expansion obligation.

We could also draw innovators into the space by leveling the playing field and abolishing the accreditation cartel. Accreditation is required for federal financial aid, but the agencies who do it are independent of the government, and their very existence is geared toward maintaining the current model of higher education. These bodies should be rebuilt with a broader base of stakeholders. It doesn't matter if higher education is sticking out its chin for disruption if its competitors aren't allowed into the ring.

98

Inflation-Adjusted Growth of Harvard Endowment vs. Undergraduate Enrollment

■ 2000   ■ 2019

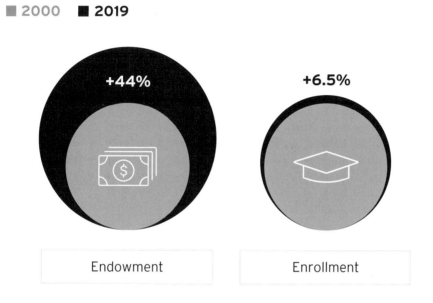

+44%

+6.5%

Endowment

Enrollment

Source: Harvard University.

Enable Other Pathways for Upward Mobility

Higher education does not have a monopoly on putting young people on a pathway to prosperity. Professional certifications that provide job-ready skills in a short period minimize the costs associated with entering the workforce. We must also embrace vocational training. When young people are trained to do the jobs society needs, they're set up for success. In America, 94% of apprentices have a job upon completion that earns an average starting salary above $70,000 in roles spanning construction, engineering, manufacturing, healthcare, and information technology. But only 3 in every 1,000 workers pursue an apprenticeship. That's far lower than the rate in comparable economies.

99

Apprentices by Country

Per 1,000 in the labor force, 2019

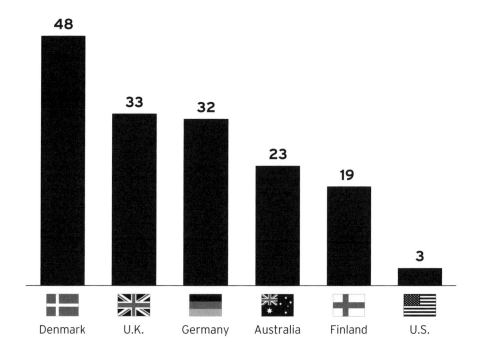

Sources: University of Oxford, Georgetown University.

Invest in National Service

Between 1965 and 1975, more than two-thirds of the members of Congress had served their country in uniform. The important legislative achievements of those years were shaped by leaders who shared a bond with society more important than their connection to politics or party. Today, fewer than 20% of our legislators have had that kind of experience.

The military doesn't have a monopoly on service. Since the founding of the Peace Corps in 1961, a quarter of a million of its volunteers have served in 142 countries.

The benefits—fiscal and social—of national service programs far outweigh their cost. Programs like Teach for America, YouthBuild, and the National Guard Youth Challenge give young adults an opportunity to serve their fellow Americans alongside their peers. The latter two especially focus on offering vocational opportunities for non-college-bound youth, an area in which we lag far behind other developed countries. We should invest in and expand these offerings and explore a mandatory service obligation.

Public service generates the empathy so deeply needed in our hyperpartisan climate. And there is demand—the Peace Corps receives three times as many applications as it has spots.

100

Annual Cost vs. Benefit to Taxpayers From National Youth Service Programs

$1.1B

$2.5B

Cost to taxpayers

Taxpayers recoup

Sources: Clive Belfield Center for Benefit-Cost Studies in Education, Teachers College, Columbia University.

Conclusion

In 1974, Hiroo Onoda emerged from the jungle on Lubang Island near Luzon in the Philippines, twenty-nine years after WWII had ended. In those twenty-nine years sequestered from everyone and everything, believing the war was still going on, he accomplished nothing. Less than nothing, really—he engaged in several skirmishes with locals, creating heartache and disruption without reason.

If the human race were to severely socially distance for twenty-nine years—a blink of the eye in history—the species would go extinct. Greatness is not only in the agency of others; anything that matters is in the agency of something else. Without relationsionships, communication, and institutions, we are not even mammals.

Human connection is elemental to something that renders everything else trivial—babies. In America, young people are having much less sex. Besides being enjoyable and (needlessly) controverisal, sex is a key action to establishing the elemental foundations of any society: relationships and families.

Before we can get to intercourse, we need discourse. And our discourse has become so coarse that our fastest-growing mediums of communication are, unlike previous advances in communication, not increasing productivity but increasing polarization and making enemies of allies. Whipped to a frenzy by manufactured controversies, half of us see members of the opposing political party as our mortal enemy.

Institutions, another key feature that distinguishes us from less-successful species, are now seen as harmful. They're no longer the mechanisms that put us on the moon or turned back Hitler but entities to be distrusted and defunded, and this is a self-fulfilling prophecy as they become less effective.

Distrust and the lack of connection have resulted in systems failures. Specifically, the central compact of any society has been broken in America. For the first time in our nation's history, thirty-year-olds are not doing as well as their parents at the same age. Young men are failing, while the old and rich weaponize tax and regulatory policy to protect their wealth and still the gale of creative destruction.

We are not just lonely—that implies a recognition that we need to be with others. We have no collective vision. We not only cannot see landfall, but wouldn't recognize it. We are adrift.

Adrift doesn't mean lost. But we can't course correct, or agree on a direction. We have the largest vessel with the most robust propulsion ever imagined, and we've registered staggering prosperity—but scant progress. We are divided, angry, and more of us feel disconnected.

However, some of the biggest clouds may be clearing. In its early weeks, the invasion of Ukraine brought new unity to the West and purpose to NATO. We saw Republicans and Democrats not just talking, but agreeing. Whether or not that unity lasts, it's a clear sign that common ground exists. Covid-19 has killed more Americans than all the combat deaths in U.S. history combined, but the science dividend may unleash a wave of well-being. Specifically, we may have pulled forward an age of discovery that takes the gift of vaccines and washes immunities over the world, liberating millions from preventable deaths. We may witness a dispersion of education, healthcare, and work from campuses, hospitals, and offices, unlocking billions of hours better spent on self-care, caring for others, or making money.

This book is dedicated to my cousin Andy, who died from complications of Covid-19 on December 23, 2021, at the age of 52. If I'd made a list of everyone I know, speculating who was at risk, Andy would have been at the bottom. Andy was a strapping, handsome man who lit up a room. Yet due to a series of unthinkable mistakes and misfortune, including Andy's decision not to get vaccinated, a beautiful nine-year-old boy is now fatherless. Like the millions of people who have lost loved ones, I gain perspective and sense the fragility and finite nature of life. But ... now what?

My hope is that the visible landfall of progress, citizenship, and perspective provide determination and direction. That we make a massive investment in younger Americans, that we re-embrace our brothers and sisters abroad, that we discern the difference between competitors and enemies, and that we recognize before all else … we are Americans. In 2021, we saw child poverty in America nearly halved. In 2022, people are booking rooms in Kyiv (on a U.S. tech platform, without intending to use them) as a means of transferring funds to Ukrainians. We are spending more time with loved ones. We are resisting tyrants, and beginning to reject polarization.

It's not a foregone conclusion that we'll get to land. We don't just wash up on any of these shores—the investment and leadership needs to be focused, and immense. However, landfall is there. It's only a matter of getting to it.

Acknowledgments

One of the profound benefits of success is getting to work with so many outstanding people along the way. This book couldn't have happened without the folks listed here. Indeed, so much of what I do doesn't happen without them. And I wouldn't have it any other way. My achievements are theirs, and I flatter myself that I've offered some small contribution to their own incredible success. Thank you to everyone who worked on this book, and to the dozens and dozens of people whose contributions are reflected in everything I do.

PROF G MEDIA

Presents

A SCOTT GALLOWAY PRODUCTION

Executive Producers

Jason Stavers

Katherine Dillon

Head of Research

Daniel Attia

Layout and Data Viz

Olivia Reaney-Hall

Chapter Illustrations

Luba Lukova

Cover Art

Tyler Comrie

Portrait Illustrations

Raaziq Brown

In Association with

Jim Levine of Levine, Greenberg, Rostan

Niki Papadopoulos and Adrian Zackheim of Portfolio

Research Team

Mia Silverio

Caroline Schagrin

Edward Elson

Claire Miller

Copy Editors

Mark Leydorf

Maria Petrova

Notes

Preface: Ballast

3 **40% of the nation's GDP:** "The Cost of U.S. Wars Then and Now," Norwich University, October 20, 2020.

3 **3.7% of our GDP:** "Military Expenditure" (% of GDP)—United States," The World Bank Group, last visited February 10, 2022.

3 **10 million service members:** "The Points Were All That Mattered: The US Army's Demobilization After World War II," The National WWII Museum, August 27, 2010, https://www.nationalww2museum.org/war/articles/points-system-us-armys-demobilization; "Research Starters: US Military by the Numbers," The National WWII Museum, accessed April 15, 2022, https://www.nationalww2museum.org/students-teachers/student-resources/research-starters/research-starters-us-military-numbers.

4 **wages began to fall:** Simon Constable, "Truman's Forgotten Economic Crisis," *Forbes*, March 4, 2016, https://www.forbes.com/sites/simonconstable/2016/03/04/trumans-forgotten-economic-crisis/?sh=f214e91c2246.

4 **went on strike:** Kristen Burton, "Episode 5 - Strike Wave," January 22, 2021, in *To The Best of My Ability* podcast, 28:43, https://www.nationalww2museum.org/war/podcasts/best-my-ability-podcast/season-2-archive/episode-5-strike-wave.

4 **Planners feared:** Sarah Pruitt, "The Post World War II Boom: How America Got Into Gear," History, May 14, 2020, https://www.history.com/news/post-world-war-ii-boom-economy.

4 **The leap forward in the human condition:** Esteban Ortiz-Ospina and Max Roser, "Literacy," Global Change Data Lab, September 20, 2018, https://ourworldindata.org/literacy.

4 **eradicated smallpox:** "Smallpox," American Museum of Natural History, accessed February 25, 2022, https://www.amnh.org/explore/science-topics/disease-eradication/countdown-to-zero/smallpox.

4 **90% of Indigenous Americans:** Chris Brierley, Alexander Koch, Simon Lewis, and Mark Maslin, "European Colonisation of the Americas Might Have Caused Global Cooling, According to New Research," World Economic Forum, February 1, 2019, https://www.weforum.org/agenda/2019/02/european-colonisation-of-the-americas-caused-global-cooling/.

5 **funded college for 2 million:** "Research Starters: The GI Bill," The National WWII Museum, accessed February 25, 2022, https://www.nationalww2museum.org/students-teachers/student-resources/research-starters/research-starters-gi-bill.

5 **Eisenhower launched:** "Traveling Interstates Is Our Sixth Freedom," *USA Today*, June 26, 2006, https://usatoday30.usatoday.com/news/opinion/columnist/neuharth/2006-06-22-interstates_x.htm.

6 **70% of Americans describe themselves:** Pavithra Mohan, "This Is Why Everyone Thinks They Are Middle Class (Even If They Aren't)," *Fast Company*, April 14, 2019, https://www.fastcompany.com/90330573/who-is-actually-middle-class.

7 **the postwar middle class:** Jim Tankersley, *The Riches of This Land* (New York: Public Affairs, 2021), 91.

8 **1,000 families:** "Love Canal: A Special Report to the Governor & Legislature: April 1981," New York State Department of Health, accessed February 25, 2022, https://www.health.ny.gov/environmental/investigations/love_canal/lcreport.htm#relocation.

8 **more than a million Americans:** "COVID-19 Forecasts: Deaths," Centers for Disease Control and Prevention, February 23, 2022, https://www.cdc.gov/coronavirus/2019-ncov/science/forecasting/forecasting-us.html.

1. Rise of the Shareholder Class

13 **"In this present crisis":** Ronald Reagan, "Inaugural Address," January 20, 1981, https://www.reaganfoundation.org/ronald-reagan/reagan-quotes-speeches/inaugural-address-1.

13 **fell from 14%:** "U.S. Inflation Rate 1960–2022," MacroTrends, accessed February 23, 2022, https://www.macrotrends.net/countries/USA/united-states/inflation-rate-cpi.

13 **Dow Jones Industrial Average:** "Dow Jones—DJIA—100 Year Historical Chart," MacroTrends, accessed February 23, 2022, https://www.macrotrends.net/1319/dow-jones-100-year-historical-chart.

Trickle-Down Tax Plan

14 **lowest it had been:** "Historical Highest Marginal Income Tax Rates," Tax Policy Center, accessed February 23, 2022, https://www.taxpolicycenter.org/statistics/historical-highest-marginal-income-tax-rates.

14 **the government owed $930 billion:** "Federal Debt: Total Public Debt," Federal Reserve Bank of St. Louis, accessed February 10, 2022, https://fred.stlouisfed.org/graph/?g=Lgqj.

14 **to over 120% today:** "Gross Domestic Product," Federal Reserve Bank of St. Louis, accessed February 23, 2022, https://fred.stlouisfed.org/graph/?g=Ls78.

15 **Chart 1:** "Historical U.S. Federal Corporate Income Tax Rates & Brackets, 1909–2020," Tax Foundation, accessed February 23, 2022, https://taxfoundation.org/historical-corporate-tax-rates-brackets/. porate-tax-rates-brackets; "Historical Highest Marginal Income Tax Rates," Tax Policy Center, accessed February 23, 2022, https://www.taxpolicycenter.org/statistics/historical-highest-marginal-income-tax-rates.

Changing Sentiments

16 **famously said that:** Gautam Mukunda, "'What's Good for GM Is Good for America'—What Should You Do During A National Crisis?" *Forbes*, June 5, 2020, https://www.forbes.com/sites/gautammukunda/2020/06/05/whats-good-for-gm-is-good-for-americawhat-should-you-do-during-a-national-crisis/?sh=c4dfde6d3bda.

17 **Chart 2:** Theodore Roosevelt, "NY Speech," Asheville, North Carolina, September 9, 1902; Franklin D. Roosevelt, "Address at Marietta, Ohio," July 8, 1938; John F. Kennedy, *Public Papers of the Presidents of the United States* (Washington, D.C.: US Gov. Printing Office, 1964), 326; Ronald Regan, news conference, August 12, 1986, https://www.reaganfoundation.org/ronald-reagan/reagan-quotes-speeches/news-conference-1; "Clinton: Era of Big Government Is Over," ABC News, accessed February 23, 2022, https://abcnews.go.com/Politics/video/clinton-era-big-government-9655598.

Declining Infrastructure

18 **1 in every 5:** "Report Card for America's Infrastructure: Roads," ASCE Foundation, accessed February 23, 2022, https://infrastructurereportcard.org/cat-item/roads/.

18 **Forty-five percent of Americans:** "Report Card for America's Infrastructure: Transit," ASCE Foundation, accessed February 23, 2022, https://infrastructurereportcard.org/cat-item/roads/.

18 **every two minutes:** "Report Card for America's Infrastructure: Water," ASCE Foundation, accessed February 23, 2022, https://infrastructurereportcard.org/cat-item/roads/.

18 **12,000 children:** Andrew Keller, "United Way Estimates Cost of Helping Children $100M," WNEM, 2016, https://web.archive.org/web/20160203004456/http://www.wnem.com/story/30995770/united-way-estimates-cost-of-helping-children-100m; Jennie Doyle, "The Flint Water Crisis - Impact, Solutions, and Repercussions," *Voices of Youth*, February 27, 2019, https://www.voicesofyouth.org/blog/flint-water-crisis-impact-solutions-and-repercussions.

18 **killing 98 people:** Lauren Leatherby et al., "Floor by Floor, the Lost Lives of the Surfside Building Collapse," *New York Times*, July 27, 2022, https://www.nytimes.com/interactive/2021/06/30/us/miami-building-missing-dead.html.

18 **spends ten times more:** Phelim Kine, "'Powerful Signal': Biden's Infrastructure Bill Sends Message to China," *Politico*, August 7, 2021, https://www.politico.com/news/2021/08/07/biden-infrastructure-bill-message-china-502739.

18 **why it takes 4.5 hours:** "Best Places to Visit in China—Book Tours and Travel Packages," China Guide, accessed February 23, 2022, https://www.chinatrainguide.com/route/shanghai-to-beijing.

18 **but 7 hours to get:** "Reservations," Amtrak, accessed February 23, 2022, https://www.amtrak.com/tickets/departure.html.

19 **Chart 3:** Josh Bivens, "The Potential Macroeconomic Benefits from Increasing Infrastructure Investment," Economic Policy Institute, July 18, 2017, https://www.epi.org/publication/the-potential-macroeconomic-benefits-from-increasing-infrastructure-investment/.

Healthcare Cutbacks

20 **In 1963, President Kennedy:** Jessica Placzek, "Did the Emptying of Mental Hospitals Contribute to Homelessness?" KQED, December 6, 2016, https://www.kqed.org/news/11209729/did-the-emptying-of-mental-hospitals-contribute-to-homelessness-here.

20 **half a million Americans:** "HUD 2020 Continuum of Care Homeless Assistance Programs Homeless Populations and Subpopulations," US Department of Housing and Urban Development, accessed February 23, 2022, https://files.hudexchange.info/reports/published/CoC_PopSub_NatlTerrDC_2020.pdf.

20 **three times more likely:** Dominic Casciani, "Crime Victims with Mental Illness Ignored, Research Suggests," BBC, October 7, 2013, https://www.bbc.com/news/uk-24420430.

21 **Chart 4:** William Fisher, Ted Lutterman, Ronald Manderscheid, and Robert Shaw, "Trend in Psychiatric Inpatient Capacity, United States and Each State, 1970 to 2014," National Association of State Mental Health Program Directors, August 2017, 41, https://www.nasmhpd.org/sites/default/files/TACPaper.2.Psychiatric-Inpatient-Capacity_508C.pdf.

Labor Loses Its Voice

22 **represented by a union:** Gerald Mayer, "Union Membership Trends in the United States," Congressional Research Service, August 31, 2004, https://ecommons .cornell.edu/handle/1813/77776.

23 **Chart 5:** "Work Stoppages Involving 1,000 or More Workers, 1947–2017," U.S. Bureau of Labor Statistics, accessed February 23, 2022, https://www.bls.gov/news .release/wkstp.t01.htm; Lawrence Mishel, Lynn Rhinehart, and Lane Windham, "Explaining the Erosion of Private-Sector Unions," Economic Policy Institute, November 18, 2020, https://www.epi.org/unequalpower/publications/private-sector-unions-corporate-legal-erosion/.

The LBO Boom

24 **In 1982, Gibson Greeting Cards:** Ann Crittenden, "Reaping Big Profits from a Fat Cat," *New York Times*, August 7, 1983, https://www.nytimes.com/1983/08/07/ business/reaping-the-big-profits-from-a-fat-cat.html.

24 **"It's kind of frightening":** Crittenden, "Reaping the Big Profits from a Fat Cat."

25 **Chart 6:** "U.S. Leveraged Buyout Market From 1980–2002," U.S. Bancorp Piper Jaffray Capital Markets Ltd., accessed February 23, 2022, http://www .pipersandler.com/piperpublic/MA/pdfs/leveragedbuyout_0503.pdf.

Productivity Soars, Compensation Stagnates

27 **Chart 7:** Josh Bivens and Lawrence Mishel, "Understanding the Historic Divergence Between Productivity and a Typical Worker's Pay: Why It Matters and Why It's Real," Economic Policy Institute, September 2, 2015, https://www.epi .org/publication/understanding-the-historic-divergence-between-productivity-and-a-typical-workers-pay-why-it-matters-and-why-its-real/#.

Income Inequality

28 **8 in 100 members:** Catherine Rampell, "The Top 1%: Executives, Doctors and Bankers," *New York Times*, October 17, 2011, https://economix.blogs.nytimes .com/2011/10/17/the-top-1-executives-doctors-and-bankers/.

29 **Chart 8:** Bivens and Mishel, "Understanding the Historic Divergence Between Productivity and a Typical Worker's Pay."

An Overwhelmed IRS

30 **roughly $600 billion:** Natasha Sarin, "The Case for a Robust Attack on the Tax Gap," U.S. Department of Treasury, September 7, 2021, https://home.treasury.gov/ news/featured-stories/the-case-for-a-robust-attack-on-the-tax-gap.

31 **Chart 9:** "SOI Tax Stats Archive—1863 to 1999 Annual Reports and IRS Data Books," Internal Revenue Service, accessed February 23, 2022, https://www.irs .gov/statistics/soi-tax-stats-archive-1863-to-1999-annual-reports-and-irs-data-books.

The Offshoring Explosion

33 **Chart 10:** Thomas Wright and Gabriel Zucman, "The Exorbitant Tax Privilege," National Bureau of Economic Research, Working Paper 24983, September 2018, https://www.nber.org/papers/w24983.

Stock Market Participation

34 **wealthiest 1% of Americans:** "Distribution of Household Wealth in the U.S. Since 1989," Board of Governors of the Federal Reserve System, accessed February 23, 2022, https://www.federalreserve.gov/releases/z1/dataviz/dfa/distribute/chart/.

35 **Chart 11:** "Survey of Consumer Finances, 1989–2019," Board of Governors of the Federal Reserve System, accessed February 23, 2022, https://www.federalreserve.gov/econres/scf/dataviz/scf/chart/#series:Stock_Holdings;demographic:all;population:1;units:have.

2. The World We Made

38 **lived in extreme poverty:** "Population Living in Extreme Poverty, World, 1981 to 2017," Global Change Data Lab, accessed February 24, 2022, https://ourworldindata.org/grapher/above-or-below-extreme-poverty-line-world-bank?country=~OWID_WRL.

38 **had no democratic rights:** "200 Years Ago, Everyone Lacked Democratic Rights. Now, Billions of People Have Them," Global Change Data Lab, accessed February 24, 2022, https://ourworldindata.org/democratic-rights.

38 **had a life expectancy:** "Life Expectancy," Global Change Data Lab, accessed February 24, 2022, https://ourworldindata.org/grapher/life-expectancy-at-birth-total-years?tab=chart&country=~OWID_WRL.

38 **had no formal education:** "Share of the World Population Older Than 15 Years with at Least Basic Education," Global Change Data Lab, accessed February 24, 2022, https://ourworldindata.org/grapher/share-of-the-world-population-with-at-least-basic-education?country=~OWID_WRL.

38 **were largely in Asia:** "Share of Population in Extreme Poverty, 1981 to 2019," Global Change Data Lab, accessed February 24, 2022, https://ourworldindata.org/grapher/share-of-population-in-extreme-poverty?tab=chart&country=East+Asia+and+Pacific~South+Asia~OWID_WRL.

39 **world's largest standing army:** Hans M. Kristensen and Robert S. Norris, "Global Nuclear Weapons Inventories, 1945–2010," *Bulletin of Atomic Sciences* 66, no. 4 (November 27, 2015): 77–83, https://www.tandfonline.com/doi/full/10.2968/066004008.

39 **cases of Pepsi:** Mark Stenberg, "How the CEO of Pepsi, By Bartering Battleships and Vodka, Negotiated Cold War Diplomacy and Brought His Soda to the Soviet Union," *Business Insider,* November 11, 2020, https://www.businessinsider.com/ceo-of-pepsi-brought-soda-to-the-soviet-union-2020-11.

Productivity Revolution

41 **Chart 12:** Max Roser, "The world economy over the last two millennia," Our World in Data, accessed February 24, 2022, https://ourworldindata.org/economic-growth#economic-growth-over-the-long-run

Billions of People Work Their Way Out of Poverty

42 **below the international poverty line:** Jack Goodman, "Has China Lifted 100 Million People Out of Poverty?," BBC News, February 28, 2021, https://www.bbc.com/news/56213271.

42 **China with wealth of more than $110,000:** David Dawkins, "China Overtakes U.S. In Global Household Wealth Rankings 'Despite' Trade Tensions—Report," *Forbes*, October 21, 2019, https://www.forbes.com/sites/daviddawkins/2019/10/21/china-overtakes-us-in-global-household-wealth-rankings-despite-trade-tensions-report/?sh=3abd87ed749e.

43 **Chart 13:** "Regional Aggregation Using 2011 PPP and $1.9/Day Poverty Line," The World Bank Group, accessed February 24, 2022, http://iresearch.worldbank.org/PovcalNet/povDuplicateWB.aspx.

Health Is Wealth

44 **Infant mortality has been cut:** Bernadeta Dadonaite, Hannah Ritchie and Max Roser, "Child and Infant Mortality," Our World in Data, 2013, https://ourworldindata.org/child-mortality.

44 **disease and war:** "Burden of Disease, 1990 to 2019," Global Change Data Lab, accessed February 24, 2022, https://ourworldindata.org/grapher/dalys-rate-from-all-causes?tab=chart&country=~OWID_WRL; "Rate of Violent Deaths in Conflicts and One-Sided Violence Per 100,000, 1946 to 2016," Global Change Data Lab, accessed February 24, 2022, https://ourworldindata.org/grapher/rate-of-violent-deaths-in-conflicts-and-one-sided-violence-per-100000-since-1989.

45 **Chart 14:** "Life Expectancy at Birth, Total (Years)," World Bank Group, accessed February 24, 2022, https://data.worldbank.org/indicator/SP.DYN.LE00.IN.

A New World Order

47 **Chart 15:** "Share of Democracies," Global Change Data Lab, accessed February 24, 2022, https://ourworldindata.org/grapher/share-democracies-bmr?time=earliest..1900&country=~OWID_WRL.

Freedom of Movement

48 **immigrants started a quarter:** Marjolaine Gauthier-Loiselle and Jennifer Hunt, "How Much Does Immigration Boost Innovation?" *American Economic Journal: Macroeconomics 2* (April 2010): 31–56, https://pubs.aeaweb.org/doi/pdf/10.1257/mac.2.2.31.

48 **immigrants founded or cofounded:** Stuart Anderson, "Immigrants and Billion-Dollar Companies," National Foundation for American Policy, October 2018, https://nfap.com/wp-content/uploads/2019/01/2018-BILLION-DOLLAR-STARTUPS.NFAP-Policy-Brief.2018-1.pdf.

48 **nearly double the rate:** Sameeksha Desai and Robert Fairlie, "National Report on Early Stage Entrepreneurship in the United States: 2020," Kauffman Indicators of Entrepreneurship: Ewing Marion Kauffman Foundation, February 2021, https://indicators.kauffman.org/wp-content/uploads/sites/2/2021/03/2020_Early-Stage-Entrepreneurship-National-Report.pdf.

49 **Chart 16:** "World Migration Report," International Organization for Migration, accessed February 24, 2022, https://publications.iom.int/system/files/pdf/wmr_2020.pdf.

The Red Blood Cells of the Consumer Economy

50 **goods carried by shipping containers:** Martin Placek, "Container Shipping—Statistics & Facts," Statista, September 23, 2021, https://www.statista.com/topics/1367/container-shipping/#dossierKeyfigures.

51 **Chart 17:** "Capacity of Container Ships in Seaborne Trade from 1980 to 2021," Statista, accessed February 24, 2022, https://www.statista.com/statistics/267603/capacity-of-container-ships-in-the-global-seaborne-trade/.

The Digital Age

52 **every minute in 2020:** Aran Ali, "Here's What Happens Every Minute on the Internet in 2020," Visual Capitalist, September 15, 2020, https://www.visualcapitalist.com/every-minute-internet-2020/.

53 **Chart 18:** "Percentage of Global Population Accessing the Internet from 2005 to 2021, by Market Maturity," Statista, accessed February 2022, https://www.statista.com/statistics/209096/share-of-internet-users-in-the-total-world-population-since-2006/.

Accelerating Technological Advancement

55 **Chart 19:** "Number of Internet Users," Global Change Data Lab, accessed February 24, 2022, https://ourworldindata.org/grapher/number-of-internet-users-by-country?tab=chart&country=~OWID_WRL.

U.S. Institutions = Genius Factories

56 **Nobel laureates in the past decade:** Kevin Nazar and Michele Waslin, "U.S. Risks no Longer Attracting Nobel-Worthy Talent," George Mason University: Institute for Immigration Research, June 11, 2019, https://www.ilctr.org/u-s-risks-no-longer-attracting-nobel-worthy-talent/.

57 **Chart 20:** "Nobel Laureates and Research Affiliations," Nobel Prize Outreach, accessed Feburary 24, 2022, https://www.nobelprize.org/prizes/facts/lists/affiliations.php.

Assisting Humanity

58 **largest provider of foreign aid:** Joe Myers, "Foreign Aid: These Countries Are the Most Generous," World Economic Forum, August 16, 2016, https://www.weforum .org/agenda/2016/08/foreign-aid-these-countries-are-the-most-generous.

58 **President Reagan directed:** Tom Guettler, "Why Ronald Reagan Was a Strong Advocate of Foreign Aid," *Global Citizen*, August 11, 2016, https://www .globalcitizen.org/en/content/reagans-legacy-on-foreign-aid/.

58 **President George W. Bush made:** Gary L. Gregg II, "George W. Bush: Foreign Affairs," University of Virginia: Miller Center, 2022, https://millercenter.org/ president/gwbush/foreign-affairs.

58 **President Obama's Feed the Future:** "The Global Food Security Act," The United States Agency for International Development, accessed February 24, 2022, https:// www.usaid.gov/feed-the-future/vision/global-food-security-act.

59 **Chart 21:** "51 Billion Total Obligations," The United States Agency for International Development, accessed February 24, 2022, https://foreignassistance .gov/aid-trends.

3. Idolatry of Innovators

62 **a decrease in church attendance:** Jeffrey M. Jones, "U.S. Church Membership Falls Below Majority for First Time," Gallup, March 29, 2021, https://news.gallup .com/poll/341963/church-membership-falls-below-majority-first-time.aspx.

63 **midwifed with tax dollars:** "The Birth of the Microchip," Longview Institute, accessed March 6, 2022, http://www.longviewinstitute.org/projects/ marketfundamentalism/microchip/; "How the Internet was Invented," *The Guardian*, accessed March 6, 2022, https://www.theguardian.com/ technology/2016/jul/15/how-the-internet-was-invented-1976-arpa-kahn-cerf; "The Invention of the Computer Mouse," DARPA, accessed March 6, 2022 https:// www.darpa.mil/about-us/timeline/computer-mouse; "Global Positioning System History," NASA, accessed March 6, 2022, https://www.nasa.gov/directorates/heo/ scan/communications/policy/GPS_History.html; "The History of Web Browsers," Mozilla.org, accessed March 6, 2022, https://www.mozilla.org/en-US/firefox/ browsers/browser-history/.

Turning Away From Community Organizations

64 **decreased tolerance of minority residents:** James Laurence, Katharina Schmid, James R. Rae, and Miles Hewstone, "Prejudice, Contact, and Threat at the Diversity-Segregation Nexus: A Cross-Sectional and Longitudinal Analysis of How Ethnic Out-Group Size and Segregation Interrelate for Inter-Group Relations," *Social Forces* 97, no. 3 (March 2019): 1029–66, https://doi.org/10.1093/ sf/soy079.

65 **Chart 22:** Ben Bromley, "In Depth: Shrinking Service Clubs Try to Reach
    Millennials," WiscNews, May 10, 2019, https://www.wiscnews.com/community/
    baraboonewsrepublic/news/local/in-depth-shrinking-service-clubs-try-to-
    reach-millennials/article_99763e68-f425-5253-875c-d6603a0c9dd9.html#tncms-
    source=login; Brian Cabell, "Are Service Clubs Dying?" Word on the Street,
    July 4, 2017, https://wotsmqt.com/service-clubs-dying; Jeffrey M. Jones, "U.S.
    Church Membership Falls Below Majority for First Time," Gallup, March 29, 2021,
    https://news.gallup.com/poll/341963/church-membership-falls-below-majority-
    first-time.aspx; "The Space Between: Renewing the American Tradition of Civil
    Society," Republicans Joint Economic Committee, no. 8–10, December 2019,
    https://www.jec.senate.gov/public/index.cfm/republicans/2019/12/opportunity-
    rightly-understood-rebuilding-civil-society-with-the-principle-of-subsidiarity;
    "443. Boy Scouts and Girl Scouts—Membership and Units," Photius Coutsoukis
    and Information Technology Associates, accessed February 24, 2022, https://
    allcountries.org/uscensus/443_boy_scouts_and_girl_scouts_membership.html;
    David Crary, "Boy Scouts, Girl Scouts Suffer Huge Declines in Membership,"
    Associated Press, June 30, 2021, https://apnews.com/article/only-on-ap-health-
    coronavirus-pandemic-7afeb2667df0a391de3be67b38495972.

Water Safety in the Richest Country in the World

67 **Chart 23:** Major Garrett and Kathyrn Watson, "Clean Drinking Water a Bigger
    Global Threat Than Climate Change, EPA's Wheeler Says," CBS News, March
    20, 2019, https://www.cbsnews.com/news/epa-administrator-andrew-wheeler-
    exclusive-interview; "Mobile Fact Sheet," Pew Research Center, accessed February
    24, 2022, https://www.pewresearch.org/internet/fact-sheet/mobile/.

Privatized R&D = Privatized Progress

68 **federal government investment:** History Center Staff, "A Brief History of the U.S.
    Federal Government and Innovation (Part III: 1945 and Beyond)," IEEE, August 1,
     2011, https://insight.ieeeusa.org/articles/a-brief-history-of-the-u-s-federal-
    government-and-innovation-part-iii-1945-and-beyond/.

68 **from a peak of 1.9% to 0.7%:** "U.S. R&D Increased by $51 Billion, to $606 Billion,
    in 2018; Estimate for 2019 Indicates a Further Rise to $656 Billion," National
    Center for Science and Engineering Statistics, accessed February 24, 2022, https://
    ncses.nsf.gov/pubs/nsf21324.

69 **Chart 24:** "U.S. R&D Increased by $51 Billion, to $606 Billion, in 2018."

College Has Become the Entry Requirement to the Middle Class

70 **college degrees are more expensive:** "College Tuition and Fees Increase 63
    Percent Since January 2006," Bureau of Labor Statistics, U.S. Department of
    Labor, accessed February 24, 2022, https://www.bls.gov/opub/ted/2016/college-
    tuition-and-fees-increase-63-percent-since-january-2006.htm.

70 **exclusive than they've ever been:** Brandon Griggs and Michelle Lou, "Acceptance Rates at Top Colleges Are Dropping, Raising Pressure on High School Students," CNN, April 3, 2019, https://www.cnn.com/2019/04/03/us/ivy-league-college-admissions-trnd/index.html.

70 **more people as a whole are attending college:** "Educational Attainment Tables," United States Census Bureau, accessed February 24, 2022, https://www.census.gov/topics/education/educational-attainment/data/tables.2020.List_2016040495.html.

71 **Chart 25:** Anthony P. Carnevale, Nicole Smith, and Jeff Strohl, "Recovery: Job Growth and Education Requirements Through 2020," Georgetown Public Policy Institute: Center on Education and Workforce, 2020, https://cew.georgetown.edu/wp-content/uploads/2014/11/Recovery2020.ES_.Web_.pdf.

The Gross Idolatry of Innovators … by Innovators

72 **WeWork filed to go public:** Rebecca Aydin, "The WeWork Fiasco of 2019, Explained in 30 Seconds," *Business Insider*, October 22, 2019, https://www.businessinsider.com/wework-ipo-fiasco-adam-neumann-explained-events-timeline-2019-9.

73 **Chart 26:** Those companies' S-1 filings.

Power Games

75 **Chart 27:** Jay R. Ritter, "Initial Public Offerings: Dual Class Structure of IPOs Through 2021," University of Florida, accessed February 16, 2022, https://site.warrington.ufl.edu/ritter/files/IPOs-Dual-Class.pdf.

The Entrenchment of Wealth

76 **U.S. households own around half:** Theo Burke and Steven M. Rosenthal, "Who Owns US Stock? Foreigners and Rich Americans," Urban Institute, The Brookings Institution, and individual authors, October 20, 2020, https://www.taxpolicycenter.org/taxvox/who-owns-us-stock-foreigners-and-rich-americans.

76 **$50 trillion U.S. stock market:** "US Total Market Capitalization as % of GDP," YCharts, accessed February 24, 2022, https://ycharts.com/indicators/us_total_market_capitalization.

76 **In 1990, it was 82%:** "Share of Corporate Equities and Mutual Fund Shares Held," Federal Reserve Bank of St. Louis, accessed February 24, 2022, https://fred.stlouisfed.org/graph/?g=LlPX.

77 **Chart 28:** "Q3 2021," Federal Reserve Bank of St. Louis, accessed February 24, 2022, https://fred.stlouisfed.org/graph/?g=LlPX.

It's Never Been Easier to Be a Trillion-Dollar Company

78 **Apple became the first:** Jack Nicas, "Apple Becomes First Company to Hit $3 Trillion Market Value," *New York Times*, January 3, 2022, https://www.nytimes.com/2022/01/03/technology/apple-3-trillion-market-value.html.

78 **each company reaching that mark:** Company filings.

79 **Chart 29:** George Maroudas (@ChicagoAdvisor), "Yearly revenue before reaching trillion valuation: Tesla: $32 billion, Facebook: $86 billion, Microsoft: $110 billion, Google:, $162 billion, Amazon: $178 billion, Apple: $229 billion," Twitter, October 29, 2021, https://twitter.com/ChicagoAdvisor/status/1454089969635663874.

The MDMA Dealer of Capitalism Is the Corporate Communications Exec

80 **"A year from now":** Andrew J. Hawkins, "Here Are Elon Musk's Wildest Predictions about Tesla's Self-Driving Cars," *The Verge*, April 22, 2019, https://www.theverge.com/2019/4/22/18510828/tesla-elon-musk-autonomy-day-investor-comments-self-driving-cars-predictions.

81 **Chart 30:** Company filings.

D.C. = HQ2

82 **lobbying in 2020:** Tony Romm, "Amazon, Facebook, Other Tech Giants Spent Roughly $65 Million to Lobby Washington Last Year," *Washington Post*, January 22, 2021, https://www.washingtonpost.com/technology/2021/01/22/amazon-facebook-google-lobbying-2020/.

82 **spent over $200 million:** Johana Bhuiyan, Ryan Menezes and Suhauna Hussain, "How Uber and Lyft Persuaded California to Vote Their Way," *Los Angeles Times*, November 13, 2020, https://www.latimes.com/business/technology/story/2020-11-13/how-uber-lyft-doordash-won-proposition-22.

83 **Chart 31:** "Industry Profile: Internet," OpenSecrets, accessed February 24, 2022, https://www.opensecrets.org/federal-lobbying/industries/summary?cycle=2021&id=B13; "Industry Profile: Commercial Banks," OpenSecrets, accessed February 24, 2022, https://www.opensecrets.org/federal-lobbying/industries/summary?cycle=2021&id=F03; "Sector Profile: Energy & Natural Resources," OpenSecrets, accessed February 24, https://www.opensecrets.org/federal-lobbying/sectors/summary?cycle=2021&id=E.

Perspective

84 **three miles above the Kármán line:** Jackie Wattles, "Jeff Bezos Just Went to Space and Back," CNN, July 20, 2021, https://www.cnn.com/2021/07/20/tech/jeff-bezos-blue-origin-launch-scn/index.html.

84 **279 billion tons:** "Climate Change: How Do We Know?," National Aeronautics and Space Administration, accessed February 24, 2022, https://climate.nasa.gov/evidence/.

85 **Chart 32:** Brian Kahn, "Jeff Bezos Got as Much Morning Show Coverage in a Day as Climate Change Got All Last Year," *Gizmodo*, July 21, 2021, https://gizmodo.com/jeff-bezos-got-as-much-morning-show-coverage-in-a-day-a-1847334966.

4. Hunger Games

88 **8 of the 10 wealthiest people in the world:** "The World's Real-Time Billionares," *Forbes*, accessed February 25, 2022, https://www.forbes.com/real-time-billionaires/#49e88cdb3d78.

88 **Elon Musk, is the richest of the eight:** "The World's Real-Time Billionares."

88 **increased their share of the nation's:** "Share of Total Net Worth Held by the Top 1% (99th to 100th Wealth Percentiles)," Federal Reserve Bank of St. Louis, accessed February 25, 2022, https://fred.stlouisfed.org/series/WFRBST01134.

88 **Income for the bottom quintile:** "Historical Income Tables: Households," United States Census Bureau, accessed February 25, 2022, https://www.census .gov/data/tables/time-series/demo/income-poverty/historical-income-households .html.

88 **$17 billion in annual content:** Elaine Low, "Netflix Reveals $17 Billion in Content Spending in Fiscal 2021," *Variety*, April 20, 2021, https://variety.com/2021/tv/ news/netflix-2021-content-spend-17-billion-1234955953.

88 **$1.7 trillion of student loan debt:** Zack Friedman, "Student Loan Debt Statistics In 2021: A Record $1.7 Trillion," *Forbes*, February 21, 2021,https://www.forbes .com/sites/zackfriedman/2021/02/20/student-loan-debt-statistics-in-2021-a-record-17-trillion/?sh=7f8280051431.

89 **Poor kindergartners with good scores:** Abigail Johnson Hess, "Georgetown Study: 'To Succeed in America, It's Better to Be Born Rich Than Smart," CNBC, May 29, 2019, https:// www.cnbc.com/2019/05/29/study-to-succeed-in-america-its-better-to-be-born-rich-than-smart.html.

89 **Sixty-one percent of kids from families:** Preston Cooper, "College Enrollment Surges Among Low-Income Students," *Forbes*, February 26, 2018, https://www .forbes.com/sites/prestoncooper2/2018/02/26/college-enrollment-surges-among-low-income-students/?sh=7134b66d293b.

89 **At thirty-eight colleges, including five of the Ivies:** "Some Colleges Have More Students from the Top 1 Percent Than the Bottom 60. Find Yours," *New York Times*, The Upshot, January 18, 2017, https://www.nytimes.com/ interactive/2017/01/18/upshot/some-colleges-have-more-students-from-the-top-1-percent-than-the-bottom-60.html.

The Great Divergence

90 **Corporate profits used to track:** "National Income: Compensation of Employees," Federal Reserve Bank of St. Louis, accessed February 24, 2022, https://fred .stlouisfed.org/series/A033RC1A027NBEA.

90 **Since 2000, U.S. airlines have declared bankruptcy:** "U.S. Airline Bankruptcies," Airlines for America, accessed February 24, 2022, https://www.airlines.org/dataset/u-s-bankruptcies-and-services-cessations/.

90 **six largest airlines:** Joseph Zeballos-Roig, "Airlines Are Begging for a Bailout, but They've Used 96% of Their Cash Flow on Buybacks Over the Past 10 Years. It Highlights an Ongoing Controversy Over How Companies Have Been Spending Their Money," *Business Insider*, March 20, 2020, https://markets.businessinsider.com/news/stocks/airline-bailout-coronavirus-share-buyback-debate-trump-economy-aoc-2020-3-1029006175.

90 **Bailouts of $50 billion:** Andrew Ross Sorkin, "Were the Airline Bailouts Really Needed?: Once Again, We Have Socialized an Industry's Losses and Privatized its Profits," *New York Times*, March 16, 2021, https://www.nytimes.com/2021/03/16/business/dealbook/airline-bailouts.html.

90 **$13 million in 2020:** Kelly Yamanouchi, "Delta CEO Bastian Took Pay Cut in 2020, but Still Got Stock Incentives," *The Atlanta Journal-Constitution*, April 30, 2021, https://www.ajc.com/news/business/delta-ceo-bastian-took-pay-cut-in-2020-but-still-got-stock-incentives/JZOBBRUFWRG2VNI4YRDR4GMEJ4/.

91 **Chart 33:** "Corporate Profits After Tax (without IVA and CCAdj)," Federal Reserve Bank of St. Louis, accessed February 24, 2022, https://fred.stlouisfed.org/series/CP/.

It's Wealthy at the Top

93 **Chart 34:** Lawrence Mishel and Julia Wolfe, "CEO Compensation Has Grown 940% Since 1978," Economic Policy Institute, August 14, 2019, https://www.epi.org/publication/ceo-compensation-2018/.

From Lopsided to Dystopian

94 **50% of Americans controlled only 2% of the nation's wealth:** "Share of Total Net Worth Held by the Bottom 50% (1st to 50th Wealth Percentiles)," Federal Reserve Bank of St. Louis, accessed February 24, 2022, https://fred.stlouisfed.org/series/WFRBSB50215.

94 **richest 1% had almost a third:** "Share of Total Net Worth Held by the Bottom 50% (1st to 50th Wealth Percentiles)."

94 **adult population accounted for 44% of global net worth:** "Global Wealth Report," Credit Suisse Group, accessed February 24, 2022, https://www.credit-suisse.com/about-us/en/reports-research/global-wealth-report.html.

95 **Chart 35:** "Share of Total Net Worth Held by the Top 1% (99th to 100th Wealth Percentiles)," Federal Reserve Bank of St. Louis, accessed February 24, 2022, https://fred.stlouisfed.org/series/WFRBST01134.

Invasive Species

96 **take 2 out of every 3 dollars:** Nicole Perrin, "Facebook-Google Duopoly Won't Crack This Year," *Insider Intelligence*, November 4, 2019, https://www.emarketer .com/content/facebook-google-duopoly-won-t-crack-this-year.

96 **1,133 episodes:** Travis Clark, "How Much Money 'Game of Thrones' Episodes Cost to Make in the Final Season, and Throughout the Series," *Business Insider*, April 15, 2019, https://www.businessinsider.com/how-much-game-of-thrones-episodes-cost-for-production-2019-4.

97 **Chart 36:** Joe Abbott and Edward Yardeni, "Stock Market Briefing: FAANGMs," Yardeni Research, Inc., February 19, 2022, https://www.yardeni.com/pub/ faangms.pdf.

The Minimum Wage Is Decades Behind

98 **In 1950, the federal minimum wage:** Dean Baker, "The $23 Per Hour Minimum Wage," Center for Economic and Policy Research, March 16, 2022, https://cepr .net/the-26-an-hour-minimum-wage.

98 **median cost of a home in 1950 was $87,524:** Emmie Martin, "Here's How Much Housing Prices Have Skyrocketed Over the Last 50 Years," CNBC, June 23, 2017, https://www.cnbc.com/2017/06/23/how-much-housing-prices-have-risen-since-1940.html.

98 **more than $15 per hour:** David Cooper, Zane Mokhiber, and Ben Zipperer, "Raising the Federal Minimum Wage to $15 by 2025 Would Lift the Pay of 32 Million Workers," Economic Policy Institute, March 9, 2021, https://www.epi.org /publication/raising-the-federal-minimum-wage-to-15-by-2025-would-lift-the -pay-of-32-million-workers/.

98 **32 million workers:** Cooper, Mokhiber, and Zipperer, "Raising the Federal Minimum Wage to $15 by 2025 Would Lift the Pay of 32 Million Workers."

98 **3.7 million people:** Cooper, Mokhiber, and Zipperer, "Raising the Federal Minimum Wage to $15 by 2024 Would Lift Pay for Nearly 40 Million Workers."

98 **$20 billion:** Bonnie Kavoussi, "U.S. Could End Homelessness with Money Used to Buy Christmas Decorations," *HuffPost*, December 6, 2017, https://www.huffpost .com/entry/homelessness-christmas-decorations_n_2276536.

98 **$90 billion:** Bill Gates and Ray Chambers, "From Aspiration to Action: What Will It Take to End Malaria?" Bill and Melinda Gates Foundation, Office of the UN Secretary-General's Special Envoy for Financing the Health Millennium Development Goals for Malaria, 2014, http://endmalaria2040.org/.

98 **every ten seconds:** Julia Glum, "The Median Amazon Employee's Salary Is $28,000. Jeff Bezos Makes More Than That in 10 Seconds," *Money*, May 2, 2018, https://money.com/amazon-employee-median-salary-jeff-bezos/.

99 **Chart 37:** Cooper, Mokhiber, and Zipperer, "Raising the Federal Minimum Wage to $15 by 2025 Would Lift Pay for Nearly 40 million Workers."

What Are Our Priorities?

101 **Chart 38:** "Consumer Price Index for All Urban Consumers: Food and Beverages in U.S. City Average," Federal Reserve Bank of St. Louis, accessed February 24, 2022, https://fred.stlouisfed.org/series/CPIFABSL#0.

Financialization and Asset Inflation

102 **America's total financial assets:** "Domestic Financial Sectors; Total Financial Assets, Level/(Gross Domestic Product*1000)," Federal Reserve Bank of St. Louis, accessed February 24, 2022, https://fred.stlouisfed.org/graph/?g=smH.

102 **a high of 5.9:1 at the onset:** "Domestic Financial Sectors; Total Financial Assets, Level/(Gross Domestic Product*1000)," Federal Reserve Bank of St. Louis, accessed February 24, 2022, https://fred.stlouisfed.org/graph/?g=smH.

103 **Chart 39:** "Domestic Financial Sectors; Total Financial Assets, Level/(Gross Domestic Product*1000)," Federal Reserve Bank of St. Louis, accessed February 24, 2022, https://fred.stlouisfed.org/graph/?g=smH.

Asset Inflation Comes Home

104 **home ownership rate in the U.S.:** "Homeownership Rate in the United States," Federal Reserve Bank of St. Louis, accessed February 25, 2022, https://fred.stlouisfed.org/series/RHORUSQ156N.

105 **Chart 40:** "Housing Data," Federal Reserve Bank of St. Louis, accessed February 25, 2022, https://docs.google.com/spreadsheets/d/16m7gXbUmm9zZHolCeqq_oT01-UwUlgG8Hrs-EWYs0Qw/edit#gid=0.

An Assault on America's Prosperity

106 **Between 1980 and 2019:** Kathryn Peltier Campbell, Anthony P. Carnevale, and Artem Gulish, "If Not Now, When? The Urgent Need for an All-One-System Approach to Youth Policy," Georgetown University McCourt School of Public Policy: Center on Education and Workforce, 2021, https://1gyhoq479ufd3yna29x7ubjn-wpengine.netdna-ssl.com/wp-content/uploads/cew-all_one_system-fr.pdf.

106 **2 out of 3 jobs require:** Campbell, Carnevale, and Gulish, "If Not Now, When?"

106 **greater than their credit card debt:** Susan Tompor, "Student Loan Debt Exceeds Credit Card Debt in USA," *USA Today*, September 10, 2010, http://www.itppv.com/documents/pdf/conversations-about-college-savings/student-loan-debt-exceeds-credit-card-debt-in-usa.pdf.

107 **Chart 41:** Campbell, Carnevale, and Gulish, "If Not Now, When?"

Another Covid Crime

109 **Chart 42:** Emmaa Dorn, Bryan Hancock, Jimmy Sarakatsannis, and Ellen Viruleg, "As US Students Return to Classrooms, Some Are Catching Up on Unfinished Learning, but Others Are Falling Further Behind, Widening Prepandemic Gaps," McKinsey & Company, December 14, 2021, https://www.mckinsey.com/industries/education/our-insights/covid-19-and-education-an-emerging-k-shaped-recovery.

The U.S. Healthcare System Is Embarrassingly Inefficient

110 **more than any other country:** "Current Medical Literature," *Journal of the American Medical Association* 108 (1937): 329–344, doi:10.1001/jama.1937.02780040079042.

110 **Sixty-four percent of patients:** Will Chase and Michelle McGhee, "How America's Top Hospitals Hound Patients With Predatory Billing," Axios, accessed February 26, 2022, https://www.axios.com/hospital-billing.

110 **charged patients seven times the cost of service:** Will Chase and Michelle McGhee, "How America's Top Hospitals Hound Patients with Predatory Billing," Axios, accessed February 26, 2022, https://www.axios.com/hospital-billing.

110 **more than $800 billion:** Terry Campbell, David U. Himmelsteinand, and Steffie Woolhandler, "Health Care Administrative Costs in the United States and Canada, 2017," *Annals of Internal Medicine* (January 21, 2020), https://doi.org/10.7326/M19-2818.

110 **GDP of Saudi Arabia:** "GDP by Country," Worldometers, accessed February 25, 2022, https://www.worldometers.info/gdp/gdp-by-country/.

110 **regulatory and administrative tasks:** Natasha Parekh, Teresa L. Rogstad and William H. Shrank, "Waste in the US Health Care System: Estimated Costs and Potential for Savings," *Journal of the American Medical Association* 322 (2019): 501–9, doi:10.1001/jama.2019.13978.

110 **more than the U.S. spends treating cancer:** "Financial Burden of Cancer Care," National Cancer Institute, accessed February 25, 2022, https://www.progressreport.cancer.gov/after/economic_burden.

111 **Chart 43:** Max Roser, "Link Between Health Spending and Life Expectancy: The US is an Outlier," Global Change Data Lab, May 26, 2017, https://ourworldindata.org/the-link-between-life-expectancy-and-health-spending-us-focus.

Waking Up From the American Dream

112 **a 92% chance of doing better:** Raj Chetty et al., "The Fading American Dream: Trends in Absolute Income Mobility Since 1940," *Science* 356, no. 6336 (April 24, 2017): 398–406, https://inequality.stanford.edu/sites/default/files/fading-american-dream.pdf.

112 **They have less than half of the economic security:** "Guide to the Markets," J.P. Morgan Asset Management, December 31, 2021, https://am.jpmorgan.com/content/dam/jpm-am-aem/global/en/insights/market-insights/guide-to-the-markets/mi-guide-to-the-markets-us.pdf.

113 **Chart 44:** Chetty et al., "The Fading American Dream."

5. The Attention Economy

116 **On January 9, 2007:** "Steve Jobs Debuts the iPhone," History, accessed February 25, 2022, https://www.history.com/this-day-in-history/steve-jobs-debuts-the-iphone.

116 **He called it a "revolutionary product":** John Schroter, "Steve Jobs Introduces iPhone in 2007," October 8, 2011, YouTube, video, 0:00 to 10:19, https://www.youtube.com/watch?v=MnrJzXM7a6o.

116 **$900 million buyout:** Saul Hansell, "Yahoo Woos a Social Networking Site," *New York Times*, September 22, 2006, https://www.nytimes.com/2006/09/22/technology/22facebook.html.

116 **called Odeo:** MG Siegler, "Twitter And Foursquare Explain Their SXSW Explosions: Hustle, Buzz, And Maybe $11K," *TechCrunch*, January 4, 2011, https://techcrunch.com/2011/01/04/twitter-foursquare-sxsw/.

116 **we spent 3%:** Lisa E. Phillips, "Trends in Consumers' Time Spent with Media," *Insider Intelligence*, December 28, 2010, https://www.emarketer.com/Article/Trends-Consumers-Time-Spent-with-Media/1008138.

116 **that number was 33%:** Yoram Wurmser, "US Time Spent with Mobile 2021: Pandemic Gains Stick Even as Growth Cools," *Insider Intelligence*, Jun 2, 2021, https://www.emarketer.com/content/us-time-spent-with-mobile-2021.

116 **Over 80% of Alphabet's revenue:** Daisuke Wakabayashi, "Google's Profit and Revenue Soared in the Third Quarter," *New York Times*, October 26, 2021, https://www.nytimes.com/2021/10/26/technology/google-profit-third-quarter.html.

116 **At Meta, it's 98%:** Rishi Iyengar, "Here's How Big Facebook's Ad Business Really Is," CNN, July 1, 2020, https://www.cnn.com/2020/06/30/tech/facebook-ad-business-boycott/index.html.

116 **bring in more than a third:** Iyengar, "Here's How Big Facebook's Ad Business Really Is."

117 **receive 70% more views:** "Mozilla Investigation: YouTube Algorithm Recommends Videos that Violate the Platform's Very Own Policies," Mozilla, July 7, 2021, https://foundation.mozilla.org/en/blog/mozilla-investigation-youtube-algorithm-recommends-videos-that-violate-the-platforms-very-own-policies/.

117 **six times the speed:** Peter Dizikes, "Study: On Twitter, False News Travels Faster Than True Stories," Massachusets Institute of Technology, March 8, 2018, https://news.mit.edu/2018/study-twitter-false-news-travels-faster-true-stories-0308.

117 **more than 15%:** Mark Travers, "Facebook Spreads Fake News Faster Than Any Other Social Website, According To New Research," *Forbes*, March 21, 2020, https://www.forbes.com/sites/traversmark/2020/03/21/facebook-spreads-fake-news-faster-than-any-other-social-website-according-to-new-research/?sh=21332c476e1a.

117 **My NYU colleague Jonathan Haidt:** Dora Mekouar, "Can Reforming Social Media Save American Democracy?" *VOA*, June 7, 2022, https://www.voanews.com/a/can-reforming-social-media-save-american-democracy-/6602408.html.

We're All Addicted to Our Phones

118 **eighty times per day:** "Average Unlocks Per Day Among Smartphone Users in the United States as of August 2018, by Generation," Statista, accessed February 25, 2022, https://www.statista.com/statistics/1050339/average-unlocks-per-day-us-smartphone-users/.

118 **about half of American adults:** Aaron Smith, "Nearly Half of American Adults are Smartphone Owners," Pew Research Center, March 1, 2012, https://www.pewresearch.org/internet/2012/03/01/nearly-half-of-american-adults-are-smartphone-owners/.

118 **feel some degree of anxiety:** "Smartphones," YouGov, accessed February 25, 2022, https://d25d2506sfb94s.cloudfront.net/cumulus_uploads/document/6u8vt576yo/Smartphones%20results,%20March%201-4,%202019.pdf.

118 **96% of Gen Z Americans:** "Who Are America's Toilet Texters? Smartphone Bathroom Habits (Texting on the Toilet Study)," *Bank My Cell*, accessed February 20, 2022, https://www.bankmycell.com/blog/cell-phone-usage-in-toilet-survey#jump2.

118 **4 hours and 23 minutes:** Wurmser, "US Time Spent with Mobile 2021."

118 **laugh seventeen times:** Rod A. Martin, "Do Children Laugh Much More Often than Adults Do?" Association for Applied and Theraputic Humor, 2022, https://aath.memberclicks.net/do-children-laugh-much-more-often-than-adults-do.

118 **about once a week:** Ryne A. Sherman, Jean M. Twenge, and Brooke E. Wells, "Declines in Sexual Frequency among American Adults, 1989–2014," *National Library of Medicine* 46 (November 2017): 2389–401, doi: 10.1007/s10508-017-0953-1.

119 **Chart 45:** "Average Unlocks Per Day Among Smartphone Users in the United States as of August 2018, by Generation."

Digital Billboards

120 **37 trillion gigabytes:** Gregory Manley, "How Much Data Is on the Internet?," *Section*, March 27, 2020, https://www.section.io/engineering-education/how-much-data-online/.

120 **within 0.2 seconds:** Amit Agarwal, "Single Google Query Uses 1000 Machines in 0.2 Seconds," *Digital inspiration*, February 19, 2009, https://www.labnol.org/internet/search/google-query-uses-1000-machines/7433/.

120 **fifth of all advertising revenue:** "Digital News Fact Sheet," Pew Research Center, July 27, 2021, https://www.pewresearch.org/journalism/fact-sheet/digital-news/.

120 **63% of all ad revenue:** "Digital News Fact Sheet," Pew Research Center, July 27, 2021, https://www.pewresearch.org/journalism/fact-sheet/digital-news/.

120 **$250 billion industry:** Sara Fischer, "Ad Industry Expected to Make a Major COVID Comeback," Axios, April 13, 2021, https://www.axios.com/advertising-industry-covid-pandemic-80c4c676-4ab5-4690-a5a7-0d897df76d49.html.

121 **Chart 46:** "Digital News Fact Sheet."

Decline of the News

122 **In 2008, U.S. newspapers:** "Digital News Fact Sheet."

122 **had fallen 26%:** Mason Walker, "U.S. Newsroom Employment has Fallen 26% Since 2008," Pew Research Center, July 13, 2021, https://www.pewresearch.org/fact-tank/2021/07/13/u-s-newsroom-employment-has-fallen-26-since-2008/.

123 **Chart 47:** "Newspapers Fact Sheet," Pew Research Center, June 29, 2021, https://www.pewresearch.org/journalism/fact-sheet/newspapers; "Digital News Fact Sheet."

Triggered

124 **55% of website visits:** Tony Haile, "What You Think You Know About the Web Is Wrong," *Time*, March 9, 2014, https://time.com/12933/what-you-think-you-know-about-the-web-is-wrong/.

125 **Chart 48:** Jonah Berger and Katherine L. Milkman, "What Makes Online Content Viral?" *Journal of Marketing Research* 49, no. 2 (April 2012): 192–205, https://doi.org/10.1509/jmr.10.0353.

Liar, Liar

126   **from 30 million to 300 million:** "Twitter, Inc.: Form 10-K," *Edgar Online*, 2014, https://d1lge852tjjqow.cloudfront.net/CIK-0001418091/2d7fa775-d6f6-4207-a469-59089b099b6b.pdf; "Twitter, Inc.: Form 10-K," United States Securities and Exchange Commission, accessed February 25, 2022, https://d1lge852tjjqow.cloudfront.net/CIK-0001418091/e38633af-2118-4b55-9ea3-97d207937321.pdf.

126   **six times shorter:** Peter Dizikes, "Study: On Twitter, False News Travels Faster Than True Stories," Massachusets Institute of Technology, March 8, 2018, https://news.mit.edu/2018/study-twitter-false-news-travels-faster-true-stories-0308.

126   **7 in 10 U.S. adult Twitter users:** Amy Mitchell, Elisa Shearer, and Galen Stocking, "News on Twitter: Consumed by Most Users and Trusted by Many," Pew Research Center, November 15, 2021, https://www.pewresearch.org/journalism/2021/11/15/news-on-twitter-consumed-by-most-users-and-trusted-by-many/.

126   **80% of all tweets:** Ren LaForme, "10 Percent of Twitter Users Create 80 Percent of Tweets, Study Finds," *Poynter*, April 24, 2019, https://www.poynter.org/tech-tools/2019/10-percent-of-twitter-users-create-80-percent-of-all-tweets-study-finds/.

127   **Chart 49:** Dizikes, "Study: On Twitter, False News Travels Faster Than True Stories."

"Political" Censorship

128   **More than 7 in 10:** Monica Anderson, Andrew Perrin, and Emily A. Vogels, "Most Americans Think Social Media Sites Censor Political Viewpoints," Pew Research Center, August 19, 2020, https://www.pewresearch.org/internet/2020/08/19/most-americans-think-social-media-sites-censor-political-viewpoints/.

128   **Nine in every 10 Republicans:** Anderson, Perrin, and Vogels, "Most Americans Think Social Media Sites Censor Political Viewpoints."

128   **Sixty-four percent of people:** Jeff Horwitz and Deepa Seetharaman, "Facebook Executives Shut Down Efforts to Make the Site Less Divisive," *Wall Street Journal*, May 26, 2020, https://www.wsj.com/articles/facebook-knows-it-encourages-division-top-executives-nixed-solutions-11590507499?mod=hp_lead_pos5.

128   **half of Americans had heard:** "5 Facts About the QAnon Conspiracy Theories," Pew Research Center, November 16, 2020, https://www.pewresearch.org/fact-tank/2020/11/16/5-facts-about-the-qanon-conspiracy-theories/.

129   **Chart 50:** "Newspapers Fact Sheet."

Fake News

130   **a sharp decline:** Jeffrey Gottfried and Jacob Liedke, "Partisan Divides in Media Trust Widen, Driven by a Decline Among Republicans," Pew Research Center, August 30, 2021, https://www.pewresearch.org/fact-tank/2021/08/30/partisan-divides-in-media-trust-widen-driven-by-a-decline-among-republicans/.

130 **the share of Democrats:** Gottfried and Liedke, "Partisan Divides in Media Trust Widen, Driven by a Decline Among Republicans."

130 **6 in 10 Americans:** Gottfried and Liedke, "Partisan Divides in Media Trust Widen, Driven by a Decline Among Republicans."

130 **at an all-time low:** Megan Brenan, "Americans' Confidence in Major U.S. Institutions Dips," Gallup, July 14, 2021, https://news.gallup.com/poll/352316/americans-confidence-major-institutions-dips.aspx.

131 **Chart 51:** Gottfried and Liedke, "Partisan Divides in Media Trust Widen, Driven by a Decline Among Republicans."

Media Fuels Misunderstanding About Crime

132 **a trend that continued:** "Federal Bureau of Investigation Crime Data Explorer," Federal Bureau of Investigation, accessed February 25, 2022, https://crime-data-explorer.fr.cloud.gov/pages/explorer/crime/crime-trend.

132 **In 20 of 24 Gallup surveys:** John Gramlich, "What the Data Says (And Doesn't Say) About Crime in the United States," Pew Research Center, November 20, 2020, https://www.pewresearch.org/fact-tank/2020/11/20/facts-about-crime-in-the-u-s/.

132 **The Brennan Center found:** Lauren-Brooke Eisen and Oliver Roeder, "America's Faulty Perception of Crime Rates: America's Crime Rates Are at Their Lowest Point in Decades. So Why Do So Many Americans Think Crime Is Going Up?," Brennan Center for Justice at NYU Law, March 16, 2015, https://www.brennancenter.org/our-work/analysis-opinion/americas-faulty-perception-crime-rates.

132 **more headline references to homicide:** Ames Grawert and Cameron Kimble, "Takeaways from 2019 Crime Data in Major American Cities," Brennan Center for Justice at NYU Law, December 18, 2019, https://www.brennancenter.org/our-work/analysis-opinion/takeaways-2019-crime-data-major-american-cities.

133 **Chart 52:** "Public Perception of Crime Rate at Odds With Reality," Pew Research Center, January 31, 2018, https://www.pewresearch.org/fact-tank/2016/11/16/voters-perceptions-of-crime-continue-to-conflict-with-reality/ft_16-11-16_crime_trend-2/.

Relationship Status

135 **Chart 53:** Sonia Hausen, Michael J. Rosenfeld, and Reuben J. Thomas, "Disintermediating Your Friends: How Online Dating in the United States Displaces Other Ways of Meeting," *Proceedings of the National Academy of Sciences of the United States of America*, September 3, 2019, https://www.pnas.org/content/116/36/17753/tab-figures-data.

6. House of Cards

138   **higher educational expectations:** Marianne Bertrand and Jessica Pan, "The Trouble with Boys: Social Influences and the Gender Gap in Disruptive Behavior," National Bureau of Economic Research, October 2011, https://www.nber.org/system/files/working_papers/w17541/w17541.pdf.

138   **Boys are twice as likely:** Laura Camera, "Boys Bear the Brunt of School Discipline," *U.S. News and World Report*, June 22, 2016, https://www.usnews.com/news/articles/2016-06-22/boys-bear-the-brunt-of-school-discipline.

139   **higher education institutions is two-thirds:** Douglas Belkin, "A Generation of American Men Give Up on College: 'I Just Feel Lost,'" *Wall Street Journal*, September 6, 2021, https://www.wsj.com/articles/college-university-fall-higher-education-men-women-enrollment-admissions-back-to-school-11630948233.

139   **men without a college education:** "Education and Lifetime Earnings," Social Security Administration, accessed February 25, 2022, https://www.ssa.gov/policy/docs/research-summaries/education-earnings.html#:~:text=There%20are%20substantial%20differences%20in%20lifetime%20earnings%20by,graduates.%20Women%20with%20bachelor%27s%20degrees%20earn%20%24630%2C000%20more.

139   **Young people in America:** D'Vera Cohn, Richard Fry, and Jeffrey S. Passel, "A Majority of Young Adults in the U.S. Live With Their Parents for the First Time Since the Great Depression," Pew Research Center, September 4, 2020, https://www.pewresearch.org/fact-tank/2020/09/04/a-majority-of-young-adults-in-the-u-s-live-with-their-parents-for-the-first-time-since-the-great-depression/.

139   **the sharpest decline in marriage rates:** Michael Greenstone and Adam Looney, "The Marriage Gap: The Impact of Economic and Technological Change on Marriage Rates," The Hamilton Project, February 12, 2012, https://www.hamiltonproject.org/papers/the_marriage_gap_the_impact_of_economic_and_technological_change_on_ma.

139   **declining marriage rates:** "Education and Lifetime Earnings."

139   **poll by the University of Virginia:** Rich Lowry, "Opinion: A Surprising Share of Americans Wants to Break Up the Country. Here's Why They're Wrong," *Politico*, October 6, 2021, https://www.politico.com/news/magazine/2021/10/06/americans-national-divorse-theyre-wrong-515443.

Marriage Rates Are at Record Lows

140   **hit an all-time low:** "Provisional Number of Marriages and Marriage Rate: United States, 2000–2020," Centers for Disease Control and Prevention, https://www.cdc.gov/nchs/data/dvs/national-marriage-divorce-rates-00-20.pdf.

140 **men in the bottom third of incomes:** Michael Greenstone and Adam Looney, "The Marriage Gap: The Impact of Economic and Technological Change on Marriage Rates," *The Hamilton Project*, February 12, 2012, https://www.hamiltonproject .org/papers/the_marriage_gap_the_impact_of_economic_and_technological_ change_on_ma.

140 **Women at lower income rates:** Greenstone and Looney, "The Marriage Gap."

140 **consistently proves to produce better outcomes for children:** Ann Meier and Kelly Musick, "Are Both Parents Always Better Than One? Parental Conflict and Young Adult Well-Being," *Social Science Research* 39, no. 5 (September 1, 2010): 814–30, https://doi.org/10.1016/j.ssresearch.2010.03.002.

141 **Chart 54:** "Provisional Number of Marriages and Marriage Rate: United States, 2000–2019," Centers for Disease Control and Prevention, accessed February 25, 2022, https://www.cdc.gov/nchs/data/dvs/national-marriage-divorce -rates-00-19.pdf.

Women Value Earning Potential in Male Partners

143 **Chart 55:** Kim Parker and Renee Stepler, "Americans See Men as the Financial Providers, Even as Women's Contributions Grow," Pew Research Center, September 20, 2017, https://www.pewresearch.org/fact-tank/2017/09/20/ americans-see-men-as-the-financial-providers-even-as-womens-contributions- grow/.

Men's Share of College Enrollment at Record Lows

144 **down from nearly 60% in 1970:** "CPS Historical Time Series Tables on School Enrollment," United States Census Bureau, February 2, 2021, https://www.census .gov/data/tables/time-series/demo/school-enrollment/cps-historical-time-series. html.

144 **more than 1.1 million women:** Richard V. Reeves and Ember Smith, "The Male College Crisis Is Not Just in Enrollment, but Completion," The Brookings Institiution, October 8, 2021, https://www.brookings.edu/blog/ up-front/2021/10/08/the-male-college-crisis-is-not-just-in-enrollment-but- completion/.

145 **Chart 56:** "Overview: Fall 2021 Enrollment Estimates," National Student Clearinghouse Research Center, accessed February 25, 2022, https:// nscresearchcenter.org/wp-content/uploads/CTEE_Report_Fall_2021.pdf.

Online Dating Apps Are More Inequitable Than Almost Anywhere on Earth

146 **The most attractive people on the platform score the largest share of matches:** Jason Kincaid, "OkCupid Checks Out the Dynamics of Attraction and Your Love Inbox," *TechCrunch*, November 18, 2009, https://techcrunch.com/2009/11/18/okcupid-inbox-attractive; Worst-Online-Dater, "Tinder Experiments II: Guys, Unless You Are Really Hot You Are Probably Better Off Not Wasting Your Time on Tinder—A Quantitative Socio-Economic Study," *Medium*, March 24, 2015, https://medium.com/@worstonlinedater/tinder-experiments-ii-guys-unless-you-are-really-hot-you-are-probably-better-off-not-wasting-your-2ddf370a6e9a.

147 **Chart 57:** Dan Kopf, "These Statistics Show Why It's So Hard to Be an Average Man on Dating Apps," Quartz, August 15, 2017, https://qz.com/1051462/these-statistics-show-why-its-so-hard-to-be-an-average-man-on-dating-apps/.

Political Divides Become Social Divides

148 **1 in 25 parents had concerns:** Wendy Wang, "Marriages Between Democrats and Republicans Are Extremely Rare," Institute for Family Studies, November 3, 2020, https://ifstudies.org/blog/marriages-between-democrats-and-republicans-are-extremely-rare.

149 **Chart 58:** Robert P. Jones and Maxine Najle, "American Democracy in Crisis: The Fate of Pluralism in a Divided Nation," Public Religion Research Institute, February 19, 2019, https://www.prri.org/research/american-democracy-in-crisis-the-fate-of-pluralism-in-a-divided-nation/.

Failure to Leave

151 **Chart 59:** Cohn, Fry, and Passel, "A Majority of Young Adults in the U.S. Live With Their Parents for the First Time Since the Great Depression."

Population Growth Is Slowing to Great Depression Levels

152 **the population grew just 7.4%:** "2020 Census Shows U.S. Population Grew at Slowest Pace Since the 1930s," *Washington Post*, accessed February 25, 2022, https://www.washingtonpost.com/dc-md-va/interactive/2021/2020-census-us-population-results/.

153 **Chart 60:** William H. Frey, "The 2010s Saw the Lowest Population Growth in U.S. History, New Census Estimates Show," The Brookings Institution, December 22, 2020, https://www.brookings.edu/blog/the-avenue/2020/12/22/the-2010s-saw-the-lowest-population-growth-in-u-s-history-new-census-estimates-show/.

Created Equal

155 **Chart 61:** Amanda Barroso and Anna Brown, "Gender Pay Gap in U.S. Held Steady in 2020," Pew Research Center, May 25, 2021, https://www.pewresearch.org/fact-tank/2021/05/25/gender-pay-gap-facts; Tara Haelle, "Girls Three Times More Likely To Self-Harm Than Boys—And Need Help," *Forbes*, October 19, 2017, https://www.forbes.com/sites/tarahaelle/2017/10/19/girls-three-times-more-likely-to-self-harm-than-boys-and-need-help/?sh=c4175827a0c5; "Preventing Intimate Partner Violence," Centers for Disease Control and Prevention, accessed February 25, 2022, https://www.cdc.gov/violenceprevention/intimatepartnerviolence/fastfact.html; Amanda Barroso and Juliana Menasce Horowitz, "The Pandemic Has Highlighted Many Challenges for Mothers, but They Aren't Necessarily New," Pew Research Center, March 17, 2021, https://www.pewresearch.org/fact-tank/2021/03/17/the-pandemic-has-highlighted-many-challenges-for-mothers-but-they-arent-necessarily-new; Richard V. Reeves and Ember Smith, "The Male College Crisis Is Not Just in Enrollment, but Completion," The Brookings Institiution, October 8, 2021, https://www.brookings.edu/blog/up-front/2021/10/08/the-male-college-crisis-is-not-just-in-enrollment-but-completion; John Gramlich, "Recent Surge in U.S. Drug Overdose Deaths Has Hit Black Men the Hardest," Pew Research Center, January 19, 2022, https://www.pewresearch.org/fact-tank/2022/01/19/recent-surge-in-u-s-drug-overdose-deaths-has-hit-black-men-the-hardest; "Suicide Statistics," National Foundation for Suicide Prevention, accessed February 25, 2022, https://afsp.org/suicide-statistics; "Inmate Gender," Federal Bureau of Prisons, accessed Feburary 25, 2022, https://www.bop.gov/about/statistics/statistics_inmate_gender.jsp.

Mass Murder Is a Uniquely Male Crime

156 **Men who fail to attach:** "Many Mass Shooters Share a Common Bond: Male Grievance Culture," *WAMU*, August 13, 2019, https://wamu.org/story/19/08/13/many-mass-shooters-share-a-common-bond-male-grievance-culture/.

157 **Chart 62:** "Mass Attacks in Public Spaces—2019," U.S. Department of Homeland Security, accessed February 25, 2022, https://www.secretservice.gov/sites/default/files/reports/2020-09/MAPS2019.pdf.

The Long-Term Erosion of Trust in the Federal Government

158 **42% of Americans believed:** Aidan Connaughton, Shannon Schumacher, Laura Silver, and Richard Wike, "Many in U.S., Western Europe Say Their Political System Needs Major Reform," Pew Research Center, March 31, 2021, https://www.pewresearch.org/global/2021/03/31/many-in-us-western-europe-say-their-political-system-needs-major-reform/.

159 **Chart 63:** "Public Trust in Government: 1958–2021," Pew Research Center, May 17, 2021, https://www.pewresearch.org/politics/2021/05/17/public-trust-in-government-1958-2021/.

Old Money, Old Problems

160 **For every dollar of wealth a typical white household has:** Ana Hernández Kent and Lowell Ricketts, "Wealth Gaps Between White, Black and Hispanic Families in 2019," Federal Reserve Bank of St. Louis, January 5, 2021, https://www.stlouisfed.org/on-the-economy/2021/january/wealth-gaps-white-black-hispanic-families-2019.

160 **Hispanic households have 21 cents for every dollar in white wealth:** Hernández Kent and Ricketts, "Wealth Gaps Between White, Black and Hispanic Families in 2019."

161 **Chart 64:** Patricia Cohen, "Beyond Pandemic's Upheaval, a Racial Wealth Gap Endures," *New York Times*, April 9, 2021, https://www.nytimes.com/2021/04/09/business/economy/racial-wealth-gap.html.

Those Funding the Future Reflect the Past

162 **Chart 65:** Richard Kerby, "Where Did You Go to School?" *Medium*, July 30, 2018, https://medium.com/@kerby/where-did-you-go-to-school-bde54d846188.

7. Threats

166 **virus one-tenth the size of the smallest dust particle:** Avi Flamholz, Yinon M Bar-On, Ron Milo and Rob Phillips, "SARS-CoV-2 (COVID-19) By The Numbers." *eLife* (April 2020): doi:10.7554/eLife.57309; "Hazard Prevention and Control in the Work Environment: Chapter 1—Dust: Definitions and Concepts," World Health Organization, 1999, https://www.who.int/publications/i/item/WHO-SDE-OEH-99-14

167 **Chinese manufacturing is dominant:** Christian Lansang and Darrell M. West, "Global Manufacturing Scorecard: How the US Compares to 18 Other Nations," The Brookings Institution, July 10, 2018, https://www.brookings.edu/research/global-manufacturing-scorecard-how-the-us-compares-to-18-other-nations/.

167 **growth of its trade network is outpacing:** Alyssa Leng and Roland Rajah, "The US-China Trade War Who Dominates Global Trade?" Lowy Institute, accessed February 25, 2022, https://interactives.lowyinstitute.org/charts/china-us-trade-dominance/us-china-competition/.

167 **Chinese skill and expertise:** James T. Areddy, "China Is Working Its Way Up From Sweatshops to Skilled Jobs," *Wall Street Journal*, Dec. 6, 2019, https://www.wsj.com/articles/china-is-working-its-way-up-from-sweatshops-to-skilled-jobs-11575464404.

The United States Retains the Title

168 **30% of the world's total:** Matt Hourihan, "A Snapshot of U.S. R&D Competitiveness: 2020 Update," American Association for the Advancement of Science, 2020, https://www.aaas.org/sites/default/files/2020-10/AAAS%20 International%20Snapshot.pdf.

168 **American startups accounting for 50%:** "The Complete List of Unicorn Companies," CBInsights, accessed February 25, 2022, https://www.cbinsights .com/research-unicorn-companies.

168 **The U.S. has more billionaires than any nation:** Giacomo Tognini, "The Countries with the Most Billionaires 2021," *Forbes*, April 6, 2021, https://www .forbes.com/sites/giacomotognini/2021/04/06/the-countries-with-the-most-billionaires-2021/?sh=35e1e458379b.

168 **bigger defense budget:** "Military Expenditure (Current USD)," World Bank Group, accessed February 25, 2022, https://data.worldbank.org/indicator/ MS.MIL.XPND.CD.

168 **quarter of the world's GDP:** "GDP (Current US$)," World Bank Group, accessed February 25, 2022, https://data.worldbank.org/indicator/NY.GDP.MKTP.CD.

169 **Chart 66:** "GDP (Current US$)"; Tognini, "The Countries with the Most Billionaires 2021"; Hourihan, "A Snapshot of U.S. R&D Competitiveness: 2020 Update"; Bryan Murphy, "Which Countries Have Won the Most Olympic Medals?" NBC Sports, February 3, 2022, https://www.nbcsports.com/bayarea/beijing-2022-winter-olympics/which-countries-have-won-most-olympic-medals; "Military Expenditure (Current USD)"; "The Complete List of Unicorn Companies"; "Global Top 100 Companies By Market Capitalisation," PWC, accessed Februrary 25, 2022, https://www.pwc.com/gx/en/audit-services/publications/ assets/pwc-global-top-100-companies-2021.pdf; Lyn Alden, "January 2022 Newsletter: The Capital Sponge," Lyn Alden Investment Strategy, January 16, 2022, https://www.lynalden .com/january-2022- newsletter; Xingyang, "The 50 Highest-Grossing Movies of All Time," IMDB, February 3, 2011, https://www.imdb.com/list/ls000021718; Mike Ozanian, "World's Most Valuable Sports Teams 2021," *Forbes*, May 7, 2021, https:// www.forbes.com/sites/mikeozanian/2021/05/07/worlds-most-valuable-sports-teams-2021/?sh=562694663e9e.

The Dominance of the U.S. Dollar

170 **Under the Bretton Woods Agreement in 1944:** Sandra Kollen Ghizoni, "Creation of the Bretton Woods System," Federal Reserve Bank of St. Louis, November 22, 2013, https://www.federalreservehistory.org/essays/bretton-woods-created.

170 **into gold at a fixed rate:** Kollen Ghizoni, "Creation of the Bretton Woods System."

170 **ended the convertibility of U.S. dollars into gold:** Sandra Kollen Ghizon, "Nixon Ends Convertibility of U.S. Dollars to Gold and Announces Wage/Price Controls," Federal Reserve Bank of St. Louis, November 22, 2013, https://www.federalreservehistory.org/essays/gold-convertibility-ends.

170 **not backed by a commodity:** "Fiat Money: Money With No Intrinsic Value But Made Legal Tender by a Government Order," Corporate Finance Institute, accessed February 25, 2022, https://corporatefinanceinstitute.com/resources/knowledge/economics/fiat-money-currency/.

170 **group of finance ministers:** Harold James, "The Dollar Wars Return," *Project Syndicate*, September 2003, https://web.archive.org/web/20060529133021/http://www.project-syndicate.org/commentary/1334/1.

170 **25% of global GDP in 2020:** "GDP (Current US$)."

171 **Chart 67:** Serkan Arslanalp and Chima Simpson-Bell, "US Dollar Share of Global Foreign Exchange Reserves Drops to 25-Year Low," International Monetary Fund, May 5, 2021, https://blogs.imf.org/2021/05/05/us-dollar-share-of-global-foreign-exchange-reserves-drops-to-25-year-low/; "Gross Domestic Product 2020," World Bank, accessed February 25, 2022, https://databank.worldbank.org/data/download/GDP.pdf.

China Has Replaced the U.S. as the Most Popular Trading Partner

172 **The initiative covers 71 countries:** "Belt and Road Initiative," Belt and Road Initiative, accessed February 25, 2022, https://www.beltroad-initiative.com/belt-and-road/.

173 **Chart 68:** "Global Trade: How to Deal with China," *Economist*, accessed February 25, 2022, https://www.economist.com/leaders/2021/01/09/how-to-deal-with-china.

The U.S. Gets Less for Its Military Dollar

174 **over a third:** "World Military Spending Rises to Almost $2 Trillion in 2020," Stockholm International Peace Research Institute, April 26, 2021, https://www.sipri.org/media/press-release/2021/world-military-spending-rises-almost-2-trillion-2020.

174 **School Peter Robertson addressed:** Peter E. Robertson, "The Real Military Balance: International Comparisons of Defense Spending," *Review of Income and Wealth* (2021), https://doi.org/10.1111/roiw.12536.

174 **America look far less dominant:** Robertson, "The Real Military Balance."

174 **two-thirds of the U.S. budget:** "Buck for the Bang: Nominal Spending Figures Understate China's Military Might," *Economist*, May 1, 2021, https://www.economist.com/graphic-detail/2021/05/01/nominal-spending-figures-understate-chinas-military-might.

175 **Chart 69:** Robertson, "The Real Military Balance."

Military Spending Doesn't Always Equate to Effectiveness

176 **tall as the Empire State Building:** "Buck for the Bang: Nominal Spending Figures Understate China's Military Might."

177 **Chart 70:** "World Military Spending Rises to Almost $2 Trillion in 2020," SIPRI, 26 April 2021, https://sipri.org/media/press-release/2021/world-military-spending-rises-almost-2-trillion-2020; "Gross Domestic Product 2020"; Dawood Azami, "Afghanistan: How Do the Taliban Make Money?" BBC, August 28, 2021, https://www.bbc.com/news/world-46554097.

Chinese Leadership in Military Drones

178 **220 drones to 16 countries:** Bruce Einhorn, Lucille Liu, Colum Murphy, and Nick Wadhams, "Combat Drones Made in China Are Coming to a Conflict Near You," University of Pennsylvania, March 18, 2021, https://global.upenn.edu/perryworldhouse/news/combat-drones-made-china-are-coming-conflict-near-you.

178 **sell for as much as $15 million:** Bruce Einhorn, "Combat Drones Made in China Are Coming to a Conflict Near You: Growing Sales of the Aircraft Threaten to Spark a Global Arms Race," *Bloomberg Businessweek*, March 17, 2021, https://www.bloomberg.com/news/articles/2021-03-17/china-s-combat-drones-push-could-spark-a-global-arms-race?sref=AhQQoPzF.

179 **Chart 71:** Einhorn, "Combat Drones Made in China Are Coming to a Conflict Near You."

Does Our Budget Allocation Align with Our Threats?

180 **enemy one four-hundredth:** Carmen Ang, "This Is How Coronavirus Compares to the World's Smallest Particles," World Economic Forum, October 15, 2020, https://www.weforum.org/agenda/2020/10/covid-19-coronavirus-disease-size-compairson-zika-health-air-pollution/.

180 **more Americans than all of our twentieth-century wars combined:** Associated Press, "US Tops 500,000 Virus Deaths, Matching the Toll of 3 Wars," *U.S. News and World Report*, February 22, 2021, https://www.usnews.com/news/health-news/articles/2021-02-22/vaccine-efforts-redoubled-as-us-death-toll-draws-near-500k.

181 **Chart 72:** "Spotlight: FY 2021 Defense Budget," U.S. Department of Defense, accessed February 25, 2022, https://www.defense.gov/Spotlights/FY2021-Defense-Budget; "FY 2021 Operating Plan," Center for Disease Control and Prevention, accessed February 25, 2022, https://www.cdc.gov/budget/documents/fy2021/FY-2021-CDC-Operating-Plan.pdf.

Erosion of the World's Most Important Brand

182 **In 1985, he declared:** "The 'Reagan Doctrine' Is Announced," History, accessed February 25, 2022, https://www.history.com/this-day-in-history/the-reagan-doctrine-is-announced.

182 **made democracy promotion central:** Evan D. McCormick, Brian K. Muzas, Andrew S. Natsios, Jayita Sarkar, and Gail E.S. Yoshitani, "Policy Roundtable: Does Reagan's Foreign Policy Legacy Live On?," *Texas National Security Review*, October 9, 2018, https://tnsr.org/roundtable/policy-roundtable-does-reagans-foreign-policy-legacy-live-on/.

182 **For roughly every 10 citizens in developed nations, 6 believe:** "Most Believe the U.S. Is No Longer a Good Model of Democracy," Pew Research Center, October 29, 2021, https://www.pewresearch.org/global/2021/11/01/what-people-around-the-world-like-and-dislike-about-american-society-and-politics/pg_2021-11-01_soft-power_0-04/.

183 **Chart 73:** "Favorability of the U.S. Is Up Sharply Since 2020," Pew Research Center, June 9, 2021, https://www.pewresearch.org/global/2021/06/10/americas-image-abroad-rebounds-with-transition-from-trump-to-biden/pg_2021-06-10_us-image_00-013/.

The U.S. Is No Longer the World's Laboratory

184 **69% of global:** "Global Research and Development Expenditures: Fact Sheet," Congressional Research Service, accessed February 25, 2022, https://sgp.fas.org/crs/misc/R44283.pdf.

184 **Moderna $25 million in 2013:** Emily Mullin, "Moderna Lands $25M Grant to Develop Its RNA Platform Against Infectious Diseases, Bioterror," FierceBioTech, October 2, 2013, https://www.fiercebiotech.com/r-d/moderna-lands-25m-grant-to-develop-its-rna-platform-against-infectious-diseases-bioterror.

184 **half-billion doses later:** Peter Loftus, "Moderna Plans to Expand Production to Make Covid-19 Vaccine Boosters, Supply More Countries," *Wall Street Journal*, June 21, 2021, https://www.wsj.com/articles/moderna-plans-to-expand-production-to-make-covid-19-vaccine-boosters-supply-more-countries-11624273200.

184 **30% of global investment:** "Global Research and Development Expenditures: Fact Sheet."

185 **Chart 74:** "Global Research and Development Expenditures: Fact Sheet."

Clean Energy's Silk Road Runs Through China

186 **Few clean energy minerals are produced or processed:** Mike Baker and Jack Healy, "As Miners Chase Clean-Energy Minerals, Tribes Fear a Repeat of the Past," *New York Times*, December 27, 2021, https://www.nytimes.com/2021/12/27/us/mining-clean-energy-antimony-tribes.html.

187 **Chart 75:** "The Role of Critical Minerals in Clean Energy Transitions," International Energy Agency, accessed February 2022, https://www.iea.org/reports/the-role-of-critical-minerals-in-clean-energy-transitions/executive-summary.

The Spawning Ground for Capitalism's Apex Predators

188 **grown from 30 to 32 in the past:** Justin Jimenez, Tom Orlik, and Cedric Sam, "World-Dominating Superstar Firms Get Bigger, Techier, and More Chinese," Bloomberg, May 21, 2021, https://www.bloomberg.com/graphics/2021-biggest-global-companies-growth-trends/?sref=AhQQoPzF.

188 **which lost more representatives:** Jimenez, Orlik, and Sam, "World-Dominating Superstar Firms Get Bigger, Techier, and More Chinese."

189 **Chart 76:** Jimenez, Orlik, and Sam, "World-Dominating Superstar Firms Get Bigger, Techier, and More Chinese."

8. The Bright Side of Instability

192 **there were eight:** Andrew Pollack, "Bell System Breakup Opens Era of Great Expectations and Great Concern," *New York Times*, January 1, 1984, https://www.nytimes.com/1984/01/01/us/bell-system-breakup-opens-era-of-great-expectations-and-great-concern.html.

192 **Sprint and MCI:** Bret Swanson, "Lessons From The AT&T Break Up, 30 Years Later," American Enterprise Institute, January 3, 2014, https://www.aei.org/technology-and-innovation/lessons-att-break-30-years-later/.

193 **30% in just five years:** Kate Ballen and Kenneth Labich, "Was Breaking Up AT&T a Good Idea?," *Fortune*, January 2, 1989, https://money.cnn.com/magazines/fortune/fortune_archive/1989/01/02/71446/.

Crises Trigger Growth

194 **killed more than 25 million people:** "Black Death: Effects and Significance," *Encyclopedia Britannica*, accessed February 25, 2022, https://www.britannica.com/event/Black-Death/Effects-and-significance.

195 **Chart 77:** Nico Voigtländer and Hans-Joachim Voth, "The Three Horsemen of Riches: Plague, War, and Urbanization in Early Modern Europe," *The Review of Economic Studies* 80, no. 2 (April 2013): 774–811, http://www.eief.it/files/2010/04/hans-joachim-voth.pdf.

Resetting Expectations

197 **Chart 78:** Emily C. Bianchi, "The Bright Side of Bad Times: The Affective Advantages of Entering the Workforce in a Recession," *Administrative Science Quarterly* 58, no. 4 (December 2013): 587–623, https://doi .org/10.1177/0001839213509590.

Surging Startups

198 **5.4 million new business applications:** Andrea Hsu, "New Businesses Soared to Record Highs in 2021. Here's a Taste of One of Them," NPR, January 12, 2022, https://www.npr.org/2022/01/12/1072057249/new-business-applications-record-high-great-resignation-pandemic-entrepreneur.

199 **Chart 79:** Kenan Fikri, Daniel Newman, and Jimmy O'Donnell, "The Startup Surge? Unpacking 2020 Trends in Business Formation," Economic Innovation Group, February 8, 2021, https://eig.org/news/the-startup-surge-business-formation-trends-in-2020.

Immigrants Are the Original Entrepreneurs

200 **greater rates than American-born citizens:** Dan Kosten, "Immigrants as Economic Contributors: Immigrant Entrepreneurs," National Immigration Forum, July 11, 2018, https://immigrationforum.org/article/immigrants-as-economic-contributors-immigrant-entrepreneurs/

200 **rate of new entrepreneurs among immigrants:** Kosten, "Immigrants as Economic Contributors."

201 **Chart 80:** "National Report on Early-Stage Entrepreneurship in the United States: 2020," Kaufmann Indicators of Entrepreneurship, accessed February 25, 2022, https://indicators.kauffman.org/wp-content/uploads/sites/2/2021/03/2020_ Early-Stage-Entrepreneurship-National-Report.pdf.

Seeking Refuge

203 **Chart 81:** "From Struggle to Resilience: The Economic Impact of Refugees in America," New American Economy, June 2017, http://research .newamericaneconomy.org/wp-content/uploads/sites/2/2017/11/NAE_Refugees_ V6.pdf.

Getting Banked

204 **a third of the world's adults:** "World Population Prospects 2019," United Nations, accessed February 25, 2022, https://population.un.org/wpp/Download/Standard/ Interpolated/.

204 **a third of the world's adults:** "The Global Findex Database 2017: The Unbanked," World Bank Group, accessed February 25, 2022, https://globalfindex.worldbank .org/chapters/unbanked.

204 **50% of adults are unbanked:** "2017 Findex Full Report: Chapter 2: Unbanked,"
     World Bank Group, accessed February 25, 2022, https://globalfindex.worldbank
     .org/sites/globalfindex/files/chapters/2017%20Findex%20full%20report_
     chapter2.pdf.

204 **4 million people:** Peter Renton, "Podcast 331: Pierpaolo Barbieri of Ualá,"
     LendIt Fintech, December 17, 2021, https://www.lendacademy.com/podcast-331-
     pierpaolo-barbieri-of-uala/.

204 **9% of the country:** "Population, Total—Argentina," World Bank Group,
     accessed February 25, 2022, https://data.worldbank.org/indicator/SP.POP
     .TOTL?locations=AR.

204 **more than 25% of eighteen- to twenty-five-year-olds:** Renton, "Podcast 331:
     Pierpaolo Barbieri of Ualá."

205 **Chart 82:** "The Global Findex Database: About," World Bank Group, accessed
     February 25, 2022, https://globalfindex.worldbank.org/.

9. Possible Futures

208 **Microsoft was a colossus:** Amrith Ramkumar, "Microsoft's Market Value Hits
     a Dot-Com Era Milestone: $600 Billion," *Wall Street Journal*, October 19, 2017,
     https://www.wsj.com/articles/microsofts-market-value-hits-a-dot-com-era-
     milestone-600-billion-1508445303.

208 ***Star Trek: The Next Generation*'s Borg:** "Boardwatch Magazine: Guide to the
     Internet, World Wide Web and BBS," *Boardwatch Magazine*, May 1996, https://
     archive.org/details/boardwatch-1996-05/mode/2up.

208 **antitrust lawsuit from the government:** "U.S. v. Microsoft Court's Findings
     of Fact," United States Department of Justice, November 5, 1999, https://www
     .justice.gov/atr/us-v-microsoft-courts-findings-fact.

Printing Our Way to Prosperity

210 **aggressively expanding the money supply:** Eric Milstein and David Wessel,
     "What Did the Fed Do in Response to the COVID-19 Crisis?" The Brookings
     Institution, December 17, 2021, https://www.brookings.edu/research/fed-
     response-to-covid19/.

210 **accompanied by inflation:** Drew Desilver, "Inflation Has Risen Around the
     World, but the U.S. Has Seen One of the Biggest Increases," Pew Research
     Center, November 24, 2021, https://www.pewresearch.org/fact-tank/2021/11/24/
     inflation-has-risen-around-the-world-but-the-u-s-has-seen-one-of-the-biggest-
     increases/.

211 **Chart 83:** "Real M2 Money Stock," Federal Reserve Bank of St. Louis, accessed February 25, 2022, https://fred.stlouisfed.org/series/M2REAL.

Drowning in Cash

212 **restaurants stopped printing menus:** "German Hyperinflation 1922/23: A Law and Economics Approach," *Germany: Eul Verlag* (2010).

212 **hundreds of political assassinations:** Erin Blakemore, "After WWI, Hundreds of Politicians Were Murdered in Germany," History, October 26, 2018, https://www.history.com/news/political-assassinations-germany-weimar-republic.

212 **seeking reparations payments:** "Reparations," *Encyclopedia Britannica*, accessed February 25, 2022, https://www.britannica.com/topic/reparations.

213 **Chart 84:** Tracy Alloway, "Some Useful Things I've Learned about Germany's Hyperinflation," *Financial Times*, March 1, 2010, https://www.ft.com/content/25f43ac1-1159-3723-a90f-94fcfc1b5276.

Investment in the Social Safety Net

214 **voted against an actual infrastructure bill:** Luke Broadwater and Zach Montague, "In Infrastructure Votes, 19 Members Broke With Their Party," *New York Times*, November 12, 2021, https://www.nytimes.com/2021/11/06/us/politics/defectors-infrastructure-bill-squad.html.

214 **leave out the brand name:** Frank Newport, "What's in a Name? Affordable Care Act vs. Obamacare," Gallup, November 20, 2013, https://news.gallup.com/opinion/polling-matters/169541/name-affordable-care-act-obamacare.aspx.

214 **20% to 30% of GDP:** "Public Social Spending as a Share of GDP, 1980 to 2016," World Bank Group, accessed February 25, 2022, https://ourworldindata.org/grapher/social-spending-oecd-longrun?time=1980.latest&country=DEU~FRA~JPN~GBR~USA.

215 **Chart 85:** "Public Social Spending as a Share of GDP, 1980 to 2016."

Smothered by the Safety Net

216 **twenty-eight of the past forty-one years:** "GDP Growth (Annual %)—United States, Euro Area," World Bank Group, accessed February 25, 2022, https://data.worldbank.org/indicator/NY.GDP.MKTP.KD.ZG?end=2020&locations=US-XC&start=1980.

217 **Chart 86:** "GDP Growth (Annual %)—United States, Euro Area."

Metadystopia

218 **spending billions to monitor:** Josh Chin, "China Spends More on Domestic Security as Xi's Powers Grow," *Wall Street Journal*, March 6, 2018, https://www.wsj.com/articles/china-spends-more-on-domestic-security-as-xis-powers-grow-1520358522.

219 **Chart 87:** "Number of Monthly Active Players of Minecraft Worldwide as of August 2021 (in Millions)," Statista, accessed February 25, 2022, https://www.statista.com/statistics/680139/minecraft-active-players-worldwide; Brian Dean, "Roblox User and Growth Stats 2022," Backlinko, January 5, 2022, https://backlinko.com/roblox-users.

Fast Future

221 **Chart 88:** Willem Roper, "Remote Work Could Double Permanently," Statista, December 16, 2020, https://www.statista.com/chart/23781/remote-work-teams-departments.

Space Is Lonely Without Friends

223 **Chart 89:** Daniel A. Cox, "Men's Social Circles are Shrinking," Survey Center on American Life, June 29, 2021, https://americansurveycenter.org/why-mens-social-circles-are-shrinking.

10. What We Must Do

227 **President Clinton famously said:** William J. Clinton, "First Inaugural Address of William J. Clinton," Lillian Goldman Law Library, January 20, 1993, https://avalon.law.yale.edu/20th_century/clinton1.asp.

Simplify the Tax Code

228 **6.1 billion hours for all taxpayers to handle their taxes:** "Most Serious Problems: The Complexity of the Tax Code," Taxpayer Advocate Service, 2012, https://www.taxpayeradvocate.irs.gov/wp-content/uploads/2020/08/Most-Serious-Problems-Tax-Code-Complexity.pdf.

228 **the government calculates taxes:** "The Tax Policy Center's Briefing Book," Tax Policy Center, accessed February 25, 2022, https://www.taxpolicycenter.org/briefing-book/what-other-countries-use-return-free-filing.

229 **Chart 90:** Scott A. Hodge, "The Compliance Costs of IRS Regulations," Tax Foundation, June 15, 2016, https://taxfoundation.org/compliance-costs-irs-regulations/.

Rebuild the Regulatory System

230 **spent roughly $18 million and $20 million:** Tony Romm, "Amazon, Facebook, Other Tech Giants Spent Roughly $65 Million to Lobby Washington Last Year," *Washington Post*, January 22, 2021, https://www.washingtonpost.com/technology/2021/01/22/amazon-facebook-google-lobbying-2020/.

230 **Amazon has been increasing:** Naomi Nix, "Amazon Is Flooding D.C. With Money and Muscle: The Influence Game," *Bloomberg Businessweek*, March 7, 2019, https://www.bloomberg.com/graphics/2019-amazon-lobbying/?sref=AhQQoPzF.

230 **has more full-time lobbyists:** Jeffrey Dastin, Chris Kirkham, and Aditya Kalra, "Amazon Wages Secret War on Americans' Privacy, Documents Show," Reuters, November 19, 2021, https://www.reuters.com/investigates/special-report/amazon-privacy-lobbying.

230 **have collectively spent $374.7 million:** "Analysis of the Fossil Fuel Industry's Legislative Lobbying and Capital Expenditures Related to Climate Change," Congress of the United States, October 28, 2021, https://oversight.house.gov/sites/democrats.oversight.house.gov/files/Analysis%20of%20the%20Fossil%20Fuel%20Industrys%20Legislative%20Lobbying%20and%20Capital%20Expenditures%20Related%20to%20Climate%20Change%20-%20Staff%20Memo%20%2810.28.21%29.pdf.

231 **Chart 91:** Office of the Inspector General, "EPA's Compliance Monitoring Activities, Enforcement Actions, and Enforcement Results Generally Declined from Fiscal Years 2006 Through 2018," Environmental Protection Agency, March 31, 2020, https://www.epa.gov/sites/default/files/2020-04/documents/_epaoig_20200331_20-p-0131_0.pdf.

Restore the Algebra of Deterrence

232 **$5 billion fine in 2019:** "FTC Imposes $5 Billion Penalty and Sweeping New Privacy Restrictions on Facebook," Federal Trade Commission, July 24, 2019, https://www.ftc.gov/news-events/press-releases/2019/07/ftc-imposes-5-billion-penalty-sweeping-new-privacy-restrictions.

232 **7% of the company's year-end revenue:** "FBMeta Platforms, Inc.," Seeking Alpha, accessed February 25, 2022, https://seekingalpha.com/symbol/FB/charting?axis=linear&compare=FB,SP500TR&interval=5Y&metric=marketCap.

233 **Chart 92:** "Facebook Reports Fourth Quarter and Full Year 2019 Results," Facebook, accessed February 25, 2022, https://investor.fb.com/investor-news/press-release-details/2020/Facebook-Reports-Fourth-Quarter-and-Full-Year-2019-Results/default.aspx.

Reform Section 230

234 **16% of Americans had access:** Esteban Ortiz-Ospina, Hannah Ritchie, and Max Roser, "Internet," Global Change Data Lab, 2015, https://ourworldindata.org/internet.

235 **Chart 93:** Prof G analysis.

Rethink the Land of the ~~Free~~ Incarcerated

236 **"pre-criminal social dangerousness":** "8,400 Cubans Serve Time for Pre-Criminal Social Dangerousness," Civil Rights Defenders, January 13, 2020, https://crd.org/2020/01/13/8400-cubans-serve-time-for-pre-criminal-social-dangerousness/.

237 **Chart 94:** "World Prison Brief Data," World Prison Brief, accessed February 25, 2022, https://www.prisonstudies.org/world-prison-brief-data.

Enact a One-Time Wealth Tax

239 **Chart 95:** "Unemployment Rises in 2020 as the Country Battles the COVID-19 Pandemic," U.S. Bureau of Labor Statistics, June 2021, https://www.bls.gov/opub/mlr/2021/article/unemployment-rises-in-2020-as-the-country-battles-the-covid-19-pandemic.htm; "House Passes The Heroes Act," House Committee on Appropriations, May 15, 2020, https://appropriations.house.gov/news/press-releases/house-passes-heroes-act.

Rebrand Nuclear

240 **A single generator:** "Nuclear Provides Carbon-Free Energy 24/7," Nuclear Energy Institute, accessed February 25, 2022, https://www.nei.org/fundamentals/nuclear-provides-carbon-free-energy.

240 **the most unpopular energy source:** Lisa Martine Jenkins, "Nuclear Energy Among the Least Popular Sources of Power in the U.S., Polling Shows," Morning Consult, September 9, 2020, https://morningconsult.com/2020/09/09/nuclear-energy-polling/.

241 **Chart 96:** Hannah Ritchie, "What Are the Safest and Cleanest Sources of Energy?" Global Change Data Lab, February 10, 2020, https://ourworldindata.org/safest-sources-of-energy.

Support Children and Family Formation

242 **1 in 7 American children:** "The State of America's Children: 2021," Children's Defense Fund, accessed February 25, 2022, https://www.childrensdefense.org/wp-content/uploads/2021/04/The-State-of-Americas-Children-2021.pdf.

242 **maternal labor force participation climbed:** Rasheed Malik, "The Effects of Universal Preschool in Washington, D.C.," Center for American Progress, September 26, 2018, https://www.americanprogress.org/article/effects-universal-preschool-washington-d-c/.

242 **2011 study by Harvard economist Raj Chetty:** Raj Chetty, John N. Friedman, Nathaniel Hilger, Emmanuel Saez, Diane Whitmore Schanzenbach, and Danny Yagan, "How Does Your Kindergarten Classroom Affect Your Earnings? Evidence From Project Star," *The Quarterly Journal of Economics* 126, no. 4 (March 2011): 1593–1660.

242 **federal child tax credit:** "Child Tax Credit Overview," National Conference of State Legislatures, February 1, 2022, https://www.ncsl.org/research/human-services/child-tax-credit-overview.aspx.

242 **do more than any current program:** Kevin Corinth, Bruce Meyer, Matthew Stadnicki, and Derek Wu, "The Anti-Poverty, Targeting, and Labor Supply Effects of the Proposed Child Tax Credit Expansion," University of Chicago, Becker Friedman Institute for Economics, Working Paper No. 2021–115 (October 7, 2021), http://dx.doi.org/10.2139/ssrn.3938983.

243 **Chart 97:** Ife Floyd and Danilo Trisi, "Benefits of Expanding Child Tax Credit Outweigh Small Employment Effects," Center on Budget and Policy Priorities, March 1, 2021, https://www.cbpp.org/research/federal-tax/benefits-of-expanding-child-tax-credit-outweigh-small-employment-effects.

Reform Higher Ed

244 **$600 billion in endowments:** "Fast Facts: Endowments," National Center for Educational Statistics, accessed February 25, 2022, https://nces.ed.gov/fastfacts/display.asp?id=73.

245 **Chart 98:** "Harvard Endowment Beats Benchmarks, Value Declines," *Harvard Gazette*, September 26, 2001, https://news.harvard.edu/gazette/story/2001/09/harvard-gazette-harvard-endowment-beats-benchmarks-value-declines; "Harvard University Fact Book," President and Fellows of Harvard College, accessed February 25, 2022, https://oir.harvard.edu/files/huoir/files/harvard_fact_book_2003-2004.pdf; "Student Enrollment Data," Harvard University, Office of Institutional Research, accessed February 25, 2022, https://oir.harvard.edu/fact-book/enrollment; Cindy H. Zhang, "Harvard Endowment Returns 6.5 Percent for Fiscal Year 2019," *The Harvard Crimson*, Sept. 27, 2019, https://www.thecrimson.com/article/2019/9/27/harvard-endowment-returns-2019/.

Enable Other Pathways for Upward Mobility

246 **94% of apprentices:** "Discover Apprenticeship," U.S. Department of Labor, Employment and Training Administration, September 2020, https://www.apprenticeship.gov/sites/default/files/Apprenticeship_Fact_Sheet.pdf.

247 **Chart 99:** Maia Chankseliani and Aizuddin Mohamed Anuar, "Cross-Country Comparison of Engagement in Apprenticeships: A Conceptual Analysis of Incentives for Individuals and Firms," *International Journal for Research in Vocational Education and Training* 6, no. 3 (December 2019): 261–83, doi:10.13152/IJRVET.6.3.4; Colin John Becht, "Apprenticing America: The Effects of Tax Credits for Registered Apprenticeship Programs," Georgetown University, Graduate School of Arts and Sciences, April 19, 2019, https://repository.library.georgetown.edu/bitstream/handle/10822/1055057/Becht_georgetown_0076M_14207.pdf?sequence=1&isAllowed=y.

Invest in National Service

248 **served their country in uniform:** Katherine Schaeffer, "The Changing Face of Congress in 7 Charts," Pew Research Center, March 10, 2021, https://www.pewresearch.org/fact-tank/2021/03/10/the-changing-face-of-congress/.

248 **a quarter of a million:** Justin Tabor, "What Does Success Look Like as a Peace Corps Volunteer?" Peace Corps, November 23, 2020, https://www .peacecorps.gov/stories/what-does-success-look-peace-corps-volunteer/.

249 **Chart 100:** Clive R. Belfield, "The Economic Value of National Service," University of Pennsylvania, Center for Benefit-Cost Studies of Education, 2013, https:// repository.upenn.edu/cgi/viewcontent.cgi?article=1021&context=cbcse.

Conclusion

250 **after WWII had ended:** Robert D. McFadden, "Hiroo Onoda, Soldier Who Hid in Jungle for Decades, Dies at 91," *New York Times*, January 17, 2014, https://www .nytimes.com/2014/01/18/world/asia/hiroo-onoda-imperial-japanese-army-officer-dies-at-91.html.

250 **are having much less sex:** Christopher Ingraham, "The Share of Americans Not Having Sex Has Reached a Record High," *Washington Post*, March 29, 2019, https://www.washingtonpost.com/business/2019/03/29/share-americans-not-having-sex-has-reached-record-high/.

250 **members of the opposing political party:** Philip Bump, "Most Republicans See Democrats Not as Political Opponents but as Enemies," *Washington Post*, February 10, 2021, https://www.washingtonpost.com/politics/2021/02/10/most-republicans-see-democrats-not-political-opponents-enemies/.

251 **parents at the same age:** Tami Luhby, "Many Millennials Are Worse off Than Their Parents—a First in American History," CNN, January 11, 2020, https://www .cnn.com/2020/01/11/politics/millennials-income-stalled-upward-mobility-us/ index.html.

Turn the page for an excerpt from
The Algebra of Happiness

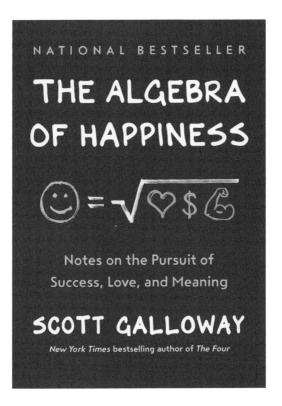

What's the formula for a life well lived? What are the elements of a successful relationship? Is work/life balance possible?

In this unconventional book of wisdom and life advice, Galloway shares his unvarnished take on life's biggest questions. With his signature humor, brash style, and no-BS insights, *The Algebra of Happiness* offers a refreshing perspective on our need for both professional success and personal fulfillment.

AVAILABLE FROM

PORTFOLIO
PENGUIN

Don't Follow Your Passion

People who speak at universities, especially at commencement, who tell you to follow your passion—or my favorite, to "never give up"—are already rich. And most got there by starting waste treatment plants after failing at five other ventures—that is, they knew when to give up. Your job is to find something you're good at, and after ten thousand hours of practice, get great at it. The emotional and economic rewards that accompany being great at something will make you passionate about whatever that something is. Nobody starts their career passionate about tax law. But great tax lawyers are passionate about colleagues who admire them, creating economic security for their families, and marrying someone more impressive than they are.

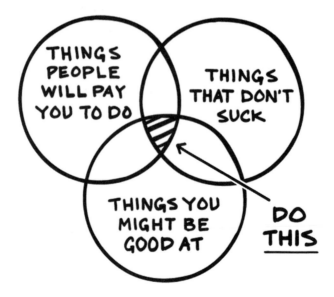

Boring Is Sexy

Careers are asset classes. If a sector becomes overinvested with human capital, the returns on those efforts are suppressed. If you want to work at *Vogue*, produce movies, or open a restaurant, you need to ensure that you receive a great deal of psychic income, as the returns on your efforts (distinct of well-publicized exceptions) will be, on a risk-adjusted basis, awful. I try to avoid investing in anything that sounds remotely cool. I didn't buy *BlackBook* magazine, or invest in Ford Models or a downtown members-only club focused on music. If, on the other hand, the business, and the issue the business addresses, sounds so boring I want to put a gun in my mouth, then . . . bingo, I'll invest. I recently spoke at the J.P. Morgan Alternative Investment Summit, where the bank hosts three hundred of the wealthiest families in the world. There are some who own media properties or a national airline, but most killed it in iron/ore smelting, insurance, or pesticides.

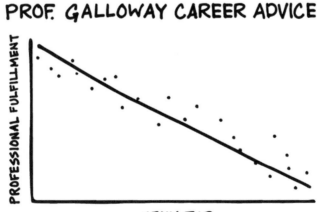

PROF. GALLOWAY CAREER ADVICE

About the Author

Scott Galloway is a professor of marketing at NYU Stern School of Business and a serial entrepreneur. In 2012, he was named one of the world's best business school professors by *Poets & Quants*. He has founded nine companies, including Prophet Brand Strategy, RedEnvelope, L2, and Section4. He is the *New York Times*–bestselling author of *The Four*, *The Algebra of Happiness*, and *Post Corona*. He has served on the boards of directors of The New York Times Company, Urban Outfitters, UC Berkeley's Haas School of Business, Panera Bread, and Ledger. His *Prof G* and *Pivot* podcasts, *No Mercy / No Malice* blog, and *The Prof G Show* YouTube channel reach millions. He has won multiple Webby and Best Business Podcast awards. Find him on Twitter, Instagram, and TikTok: @profgalloway

If you enjoyed *Adrift: America in 100 Charts*, there's more from Scott Galloway . . .

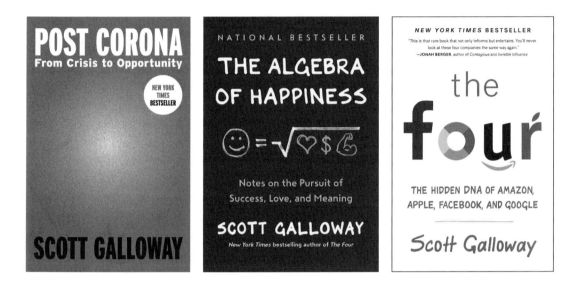

Scott's weekly, Webby Award–winning newsletter "No Mercy / No Malice" has over 220,000 subscribers and features Scott's unique blend of personal narrative and provocative business insights. Sign up at **profgalloway.com**.

Pivot is Scott's twice-weekly podcast with Kara Swisher, where they break down the latest business and tech news. *Pivot* has won multiple podcast awards, including a Webby Award for Best Business Podcast and *Adweek*'s Thought Leadership Podcast of the Year award.

The Prof G Pod features Scott's insights about business and careers, as well as weekly, long-form interviews with blue-flame thinkers.

Hire Scott to speak at your event at **profgmedia.com/speaking**

profgmedia.com